Alive

GROWING IN YOUR RELATIONSHIP WITH JESUS

LIFEWAY WOMEN

Lifeway Press®
Brentwood, Tennessee

Published by Lifeway Press® • © 2024 Lifeway Christian Resources •
Brentwood, TN

No part of this book may be reproduced or transmitted in any form
or by any means, electronic or mechanical, including photocopying
and recording, or by any information storage or retrieval system,
except as may be expressly permitted in writing by the publisher.
Requests for permission should be addressed in writing to Lifeway
Press®; 200 Powell Place, Suite 100, Brentwood, TN 37027-7707.

ISBN: 978-1-0877-8893-7
Item: 005843020
Dewey decimal classification: 248.843
Subject headings: CHRISTIAN LIFE \ WOMEN \ DOCTRINAL
THEOLOGY

Unless indicated otherwise, all Scripture taken from the Christian
Standard Bible®, Copyright © 2020 by Holman Bible Publishers.
Used by permission. Christian Standard Bible® and CSB® are
federally registered trademarks of Holman Bible Publishers.
Scripture quotations marked ESV are from The Holy Bible, English
Standard Version® (ESV®). Copyright © 2001 by Crossway, a
publishing ministry of Good News Publishers. All rights reserved.
The ESV text may not be quoted in any publication made available
to the public by a Creative Commons license. The ESV may
not be translated in whole or in part into any other language.
ESV Text Edition: 2016.

To order additional copies of this resource, write to Lifeway
Resources Customer Service; 200 Powell Place, Suite 100,
Brentwood, TN 37027-7707; order online at
www.lifeway.com; fax 615.251.5933; phone toll free 800.458.2772; or
email orderentry@lifeway.com.

Printed in the United States of America

Lifeway Women Bible Studies • Lifeway Resources •
200 Powell Place, Suite 100, Brentwood, TN 37027-7707

**EDITORIAL TEAM,
LIFEWAY WOMEN
BIBLE STUDIES**

Becky Loyd
*Director,
Lifeway Women*

Tina Boesch
Manager

Chelsea Waack
Production Leader

Laura Magness
Managing Editor

Mike Wakefield
Content Editor

Sarah Kilgore
Production Editor

Lauren Ervin
Art Director

Sarah Hobbs
Graphic Designer

CONTENTS

HOW TO USE THIS STUDY

WELCOME! We're so glad you've picked up this book. *Alive: Growing in Your Relationship with Jesus* is a 5-week Bible study on the basics of the Christian faith. Over the course of the study, you'll learn what it means to be alive in Christ—the beautiful reality of how Jesus changes everything—and how to walk out your faith as an individual and as part of the body of Christ—the church. Here's a look at what you can expect.

GETTING STARTED

Because we believe discipleship happens best in community, we encourage you to do this study together in a group setting. Or, if you're doing this alone, consider enlisting a friend or two to go through it at the same time. This will give you study friends to pray with and connect with over coffee or through text or email so you can chat about what you're learning.

PERSONAL STUDY

Each week of this study is divided into five days, but we encourage you to take it at your own pace. As you study, you'll encounter guided reading of Bible passages, teachings to help you understand what you've read, and questions that encourage you to engage with the Bible and apply its truths to your life.

REFLECTION PAGES

At the end of each week, you'll find a place for you to reflect on what you've experienced in the previous days of study. This is a space for you to journal, gather your thoughts and note lingering questions, and take notes from your group time.

ICON KEY

 Bible Facts

 Study Tips

 Key Words

 Bible Characters

ICONS

When you see these icons pop up, be on the lookout for background information and study tips that will be useful if you're new to Bible study.

LEADING A GROUP?

A free leader guide PDF is available for download at **lifeway.com/alive**. The leader guide offers several tips and helps, along with discussion guides for each week.

FREE DOWNLOADS

Resources are available to help you promote the study in your church or neighborhood, including: invitation card, promotional poster, bulletin insert, and PowerPoint® template. You'll find these and more at **lifeway.com/alive**.

BIBLE STUDY TIPS & RESOURCES

We believe Bible study should be awe-inspiring, not overwhelming. But we know it might not feel that way for you yet. Throughout this study you'll find tips and insights to guide you, but here are a few things it's helpful to know from the start.

HOW TO STUDY THE BIBLE

There are many ways to study the Bible, but this study follows an approach known as *inductive Bible study*. Each day you'll be prompted to:

OBSERVE—Examine what the text says.

INTERPRET— Ask yourself what the text means and learn from the teaching of others.

APPLY—Take what you've learned in the text and apply it to your life.

Through this study rhythm you'll learn to mine God's Word for all the truth, encouragement, and wisdom it holds.

READING A BIBLE REFERENCE

GENESIS 1:1   BOOK CHAPTER : VERSE

When you see "a" or "b" in a Bible verse reference (such as Genesis 1:1a), it's referring to the first half or thought in the verse (a) or the second half or thought in the verse (b).

FREE RESOURCES FOR BIBLE STUDY

Thankfully, centuries of Bible students have come before you and done a lot of the hard work of study. Take advantage of that! Among the many tools available, we recommend bookmarking the following online sites to aid in your study:

- The Lifeway Women Blog: women.lifeway.com
- An online, searchable Bible like biblegateway.com or bible.com
- Biblehub.com, which makes comparing Bible translations quick and easy
- A good online dictionary, such as merriam-webster.com

Most importantly, please don't go it alone! Join a local church if you aren't already part of one. Participate in their small group or discipleship opportunities, and find someone who can walk with you as you grow in your faith.

STUDY TOOLS WORTH INVESTING IN

As you're able to grow your Bible study tool set, we recommend making sure you have the following:

- Study Bible, like the CSB Study Bible
- A Bible dictionary
- Journal
- A set of book of the Bible tabs to help you quickly locate Bible books
- Highlighter/pen set

A NOTE ON BIBLE TRANSLATIONS

The Bible, originally written in Hebrew, Aramaic, and Greek, has been translated into English many times. This study will primarily use the Christian Standard Bible (CSB) translation. But reading the same passage of Scripture from more than one translation is a helpful study tool, and you can find these translations and others on a Bible app or websites such as **biblegateway.com** or **biblehub.com**

INTRODUCTION

During His time on earth, Jesus summed up His reason for leaving heaven and coming to earth in one simple statement: "I have come so that they may have life and have it in abundance" (John 10:10). The "they" Jesus was talking about is you and me, among many others. Abundant life with Christ is the beautiful promise Jesus offers to those who put their faith in Him.

But what does life with Christ really mean? What does it mean to be spiritually dead? How does being alive in Christ affect who we are, the way we live our days, or our hope for tomorrow? Whether you're new to the faith or have been a Christian so long it's hard to remember your life before Christ, these are important questions for you to think through, and they form the backbone of this Bible study.

Beginning in Week One with the good news of the gospel—the miraculous change that moves us from spiritual death to life when we place our faith in Jesus—we'll walk together through five weeks of study that unpack the basic, fundamental beliefs and instructions of the Christian faith. We'll consider what it means to be Christians as individuals and as members of the Christian community—the church.

If this is your first Bible study, we are thrilled for you! Studying God's Word helps us to know Him and hear from Him, fills us with hope for the future, and shapes us to live like Him today. And it's a practice that only grows richer over time. We know it can be overwhelming though. The Bible is a long, ancient book, and there's a lot going on in its pages. We've designed this study specifically with you in mind, so you'll find tips and extra insights along the way to help you better understand how to study and what you're reading.

As much as Christianity can feel overwhelming, it is wonderfully simple at heart:

Jesus loves me, this I know, for the Bible tells me so.
Little ones to Him belong; they are weak, but He is strong.

The words of this children's song couldn't be more true. Jesus loves you, which you know to be true because it says so in the Bible, God's true and trustworthy Word. You belong to Jesus, and He is your strength. What is more beautiful and encouraging than this?

Laura Magness

Transformation
FROM DEATH TO LIFE

But God, who is rich in mercy, because of his great
love that he had for us, made us alive with Christ
even though we were dead in trespasses.
You are saved by grace!

EPHESIANS 2:4-5

The Bible tells one big story about how God's perfect creation was broken by sin and the lengths God takes (and is taking) to draw people back to Him. This first week of study explores the miraculous change that takes place when we realize our sinful state, turn back to God, and place our faith in Jesus Christ.

DAY 01

CREATED IN GOD'S IMAGE

by Jaclyn S. Parrish

Y ou are like God. The Bible begins with the shocking, scandalous claim that humans, male and female, are made "in the image" of God—much the same way that someone might say you're the "spitting image" of your mother. No, we are not all-powerful or all-knowing or universally present throughout all of time (all things that are true about God!). Nevertheless, you and every beautiful, horrible, ornery, ridiculous human being you know were created to be like Him. What better place to begin our study than by considering who God is and how we're created to be like Him?

LOOK UP GENESIS 1:1—THE FIRST BOOK, CHAPTER, AND VERSE IN YOUR BIBLE. Read through all of Genesis chapters 1 and 2. As you read, circle every verb associated with God in Genesis 1–2. List here some of the words you circled.

THE BOOK OF GENESIS

"The book of Genesis is the great book of beginnings in the Bible. True to the meanings of its Hebrew and Greek names (Hb bere'shith, 'In Beginning' [based on 1:1]; Gk Geneseos, 'Of Birth' [based on 2:4]), Genesis permits us to view the beginning of a multitude of realities that shape our daily existence."[1]

The Bible begins with God's story of creation. In its opening chapters, we read along as God makes, fashions, and forms. He speaks and blesses. He gives, names, and controls. And over and over again, He calls His work "good." He is most insistent upon that point, repeating it again and again: "This is good! This is good! This is very, very good!"

God spoke beautiful and fascinating things into existence, finishing with humanity. Then He urged His created humans to do the same.

READ BACK OVER GENESIS 1:26-28. What was Adam and Eve's "work assignment" from God?

These passages tell us that God placed His creation under the command of humans. But that "rule," that "dominion," was not the kind of rule tyrants wield over sycophants. It was the kind of rule gardeners exercise over gardenias. Like the first humans, you were made to cultivate creation, to care for it, to fashion new and exciting things from it, and to turn to those around you and say, "This is good! Take it, taste it, enjoy it. It is so very, very good!"

> How might your work—schoolwork, housework, hobbies, 9-to-5—look different if you approached it as an opportunity to reflect the beauty of God's creation to others? Think of at least one specific example.

Rest Like God

The Bible regularly tells us to follow God's pattern for work and rest. It's even one of the Ten Commandments given to us in Exodus 20:8-11.

READ GENESIS 2:1-3 AGAIN.

Up until this point in the creation narrative, our God was a busy God, a working God. Then, as the work of creation drew to a close, God rested. Later passages in the Bible make explicit what is implied in Genesis 2:1-3: We are made in the image of a resting God, and therefore, we must rest. But how do we rest like God rests? He doesn't grow weary. He doesn't need sleep. His constant, conscious, sustaining power is what holds all reality in existence. God did not cease being God in Genesis 2:2. So what was He doing?

> **READ BACK OVER GENESIS 1:26-31 ONE MORE TIME.** What was the last thing God did before He rested?

Observe the full sweep of Genesis 1. God began the universe with a flurry of activity, flinging stars in their places, carving mountains from the deep, braiding vines into jungles. Then, with a final flourish, He spread His arms out to His new creation and empowered humanity to go garden, to steward what He made.

Biblical scholar Allen P. Ross reminds us that the Hebrew word for rest in this passage "is not a word that refers to remedying exhaustion after a tiring week of work. Rather, it describes the enjoyment of accomplishment, the celebration of completion."[2] If God's work is the joyful work of pouring good things out into reality, then God's rest is the thankful rest of drinking those good things in.

> My guess is you don't truly feel at rest often (sleep not included). How does this idea change when you think about it as an opportunity to delight and find peace in the good others (God or humans) have made?

Genesis 1–2 sets in motion the natural rhythm of human life: work and rest, giving and receiving, offering good to others and accepting good from others. But of course, we don't carry this rhythm as we should. We'll deal with what went wrong tomorrow, but you don't need me to tell you that the world is not as it should be. Work that should be enjoyable and fun is exhausting and thankless. Rest that should be peaceful and serene is frenetic and lonely. But choosing to follow Christ means choosing to reenter this dance of giving and receiving, to relearn the rhythm of Genesis 1–2.

> Consider these two "beats" of the rhythm of giving and receiving. Which one is more difficult for you to do, give or receive? What does that tell you about yourself? About your relationship with God?

If giving is more difficult, then look for a way today to make something good and offer it to someone else. If receiving is more difficult, then make time today to enjoy something good, receiving it as a gift.

Close your study in prayer. Praise God for His creativity and the intentionality behind His creation, and ask Him for eyes to see the beauty today. Delight in the ways He has created you in His image, and pray for a growing awareness of the purpose He has for you.

BROKEN BY SIN

by Mary C. Wiley

have my mother's eyes and my father's distinct nose. I also inherited my dad's love of books and, shockingly, all of my mom's parenting phrases that I swore I'd never use, like "make good choices" and "always take the high road."

I have both inherited traits and learned traits; those I was born with and those I have actively adopted into my own behavior, for better or worse. You could say I inherited some and enacted others, choosing to practice them.

If you know one or both of your birth parents, what are some traits you have inherited from your family's genes? What have you enacted or chosen to follow from the examples set for you in childhood?

INHERITED	ENACTED

So much of our lives are determined by what we have inherited from our families, whether we can recognize these things or not. Unfortunately, "the Carlisle nose" isn't the only thing I inherited from my father. Passed down from generation to generation, reaching all the way back to the garden of Eden, I have inherited sinfulness—and so have you.

 THE GARDEN OF EDEN

The garden of Eden (Genesis 2) is the place where Adam and Eve, the first humans, lived. It is believed to have been located in the Tigris-Euphrates area of Mesopotamia. The garden included two trees—the tree of life and the tree of the knowledge of good and evil. Adam and Eve were banned from Eden after they listened to the serpent (Satan) instead of listening to God.[3]

Pick up where you left off yesterday in the book of Genesis.

READ GENESIS 3:1-7.

What question did the serpent ask to tempt Eve in verse 1?

What about the fruit convinced Eve she should eat it?

After God created Adam and Eve, He gave them one rule: don't eat from the tree of the knowledge of good and evil. That's it. Everything else was fair game. However, if they did eat from it, the consequence would be certain death. (Go back and read Genesis 2:15-17 for this context.) However, the serpent assured Eve that was not the case, that God was just holding back a good thing from her, and the fruit was actually good for her because it would make her more like God!

What immediately happened after Adam and Eve ate the fruit? Have you ever had a similar response when you sinned?

Eve was enticed by the serpent's temptation, and her trust in God wavered with catastrophic results. In a single moment, Adam and Eve's rebellion changed everything. While their bodies didn't immediately die, their close relationship with God did, and their physical death became an imminent reality. All the joyous life with God they had experienced was overtaken by shame. Sin entered the world, breaking God's perfect creation, and generation after generation has inherited it. Nothing is as it should be.

THE LETTER TO THE ROMANS

Romans is the sixth book in the New Testament and was written by the apostle Paul. Apostles were those taught and/or sent out directly by Jesus. Paul's conversion from a persecutor of Christians to one of the early church's most influential leaders is recorded in the book of Acts. His letter to the Roman house churches is considered one of the most thorough descriptions of our salvation and its impact on our lives. In total, Paul wrote thirteen New Testament letters.[4,5]

Righteous

Acting in accord with divine or moral law: free from guilt or sin.[6]

Flip to the New Testament and find the book of Romans. (Your Bible will have an index of Bible books with page numbers toward the front if you need guidance.) Then **READ ROMANS 3:10-20.**

This is uplifting, isn't it? But it's critical we understand that no one has escaped inheriting sin from Adam and Eve. My two-year-old never had to be taught how to take her friend's toy, or to demand her way by stomping her foot and screaming. It's like she came pre-programmed. And in fact, she did. As all of us are—prone to sin from the moment our lives begin. Just as this passage says, there is not one person who is righteous, not even one (v. 10).

This passage holds strong words about what sin is and what is true about humanity and their sin. How would you define sin with these verses and personal experience in mind?

What does this passage reveal about our sinfulness?

When I teach the kids at my church about sin, we always define sin as "anything we do, think, or say that God tells us not to do, think, or say; or anything we don't do, think, or say that God tells us to do, think, or say in His Word." That's a lot of words to simply say that sin is rebelling against God and His good plan for us. As alluded to earlier, we 1) are born with a sinful nature that desires our own way rather than God's; and 2) choose to sin as we walk through our days.

Yesterday, we read God's rule about following His example of rest, which is one of His Ten Commandments (the foundational law for the people of God from the Old Testament). Paul has God's law in mind in Romans 3. God gave His children rules, not because He is an impossible-to-please dictator, but so that His people might flourish and have abundant relationships with Him. He gave His children instructions because He loves them and wants life for them. However, we can't keep the rules—we disobey. We sin. And just as sin separated Adam and Eve from God, it also separates us from Him.

Thankfully, God knew this would be the case. Although we are incapable of being sinless while we live in this broken world, God has provided a way to fix our relationship with Him so that it is no longer broken.

> **NOW READ ROMANS 5:12-21.** Compare and contrast how this text describes Adam (the "one man" of verse 12) and Jesus Christ ("the Coming One").

WHAT WE HAVE IN ADAM	WHAT WE HAVE IN CHRIST

Think about the world around you and your present circumstances. What evidence do you see of sin?

What evidence do you see of God's grace because of your life in Jesus? What hope do you now have that you didn't have before?

Spend some time in prayer. Begin with a time of confession, acknowledging your sin and asking God for forgiveness and mercy. Then take time to praise Him for the total forgiveness you have in Jesus.

BOUGHT
BY JESUS

by Mary C. Wiley

My childhood church sang a song I found deeply unsettling because it asked the question, "Are you washed in the blood of the Lamb?" Every time we sang it, I'd make a gagging sound only loud enough for those sitting beside me to hear. I had no desire to be washed in anything other than warm, clean bath water. I didn't even want to see this blood we talked about so often, much less be washed in it.

However, no amount of queasiness changes the fact that blood is central to our faith and was central to God's work of redemption from the beginning. Blood is the source of life for every living thing, and as we'll see today, Jesus's blood is the source of spiritual life for all who believe in Him. Hebrews 9:22 says, "According to the law almost everything is purified with blood, and without the shedding of blood there is no forgiveness."

The Law

The Law is considered the Bible books of Genesis to Deuteronomy, with the bulk of instruction from God given in Leviticus and Deuteronomy.

Before the birth of Jesus, God had a covenant (known as the old covenant or Mosaic law) with His people that was made up of more than six hundred law, including the Ten Commandments. Yesterday we considered how everyone sins, and because of sin it was impossible for anyone to obey all those rules at once. So, as payment for sins, God specified that people had to take a spotless animal to the temple for the priest to slaughter and burn on the altar of the LORD. The offering's blood would count as payment for their sin, and then their relationship with God would be restored. This was an exhausting, smelly, temporary, and repetitive way to deal with sin. But it wouldn't always be that way.

READ THE FOLLOWING FROM JEREMIAH 31:31-34,

31"Look, the days are coming"—this is the LORD's declaration—"when I will make a new covenant with the house of Israel and with the house of Judah. 32This one will not be like the covenant I made with their ancestors on the day I took them by the hand to lead them out of the land of Egypt—my covenant that they broke even though I am their master"—the LORD's declaration. 33"Instead, this is the covenant I will make with the house of Israel after those days"—the LORD's declaration. "I will put my teaching within them and write it on their hearts. I will be their God, and they will be my people. 34No longer will one teach his neighbor or his brother, saying, 'Know the LORD,' for they will all know me, from the least to the greatest of them"—this is the LORD's declaration. "For I will forgive their iniquity and never again remember their sin."

Jeremiah was a prophet who spoke to people on God's behalf about six hundred years before Jesus came, so he and the people around him lived under the old covenant, the Law of Moses you can read about in Exodus.[8] Yet, he looked forward to a day when God would make a new covenant with His people.

> **From these verses in Jeremiah 31, what do you learn about how this new covenant would be different from the old covenant?**

Trinity

The "theological term used to define God as an undivided unity expressed in the threefold nature of God the Father, God the Son, and God the Holy Spirit."[9]

The old covenant was a never-ending cycle of failure and forgiveness because perfect obedience to God's laws was impossible for sinful humans. Our rebellion against God's ways set us in opposition to Him and separated us from Him. Thankfully, it didn't keep Him from loving us and providing a new way for us to be reconciled to Him. The new covenant Jeremiah described looked forward to the life, death, and resurrection of Jesus. Because Jesus is the Son of God, one Person of the Holy Trinity, He was able to be the perfect, sinless human we could never be.

As you **READ ROMANS 5:6,** printed below, <u>underline</u> the words that describe what was true about you. (Circle) what Jesus did for you.

For while we were still helpless, at the right time, Christ died for the ungodly.

What a gift!

Turn to the book of Hebrews, toward the back of your Bible, and find Hebrews 9. **READ HEBREWS 9:11-15 AND HEBREWS 9:24-28.** How many times do the words *one/once* appear in these verses from Hebrews 9?

Hebrews is a beautiful book that compares the old covenant to the new (the relationship God has with His people through Jesus), helping the reader understand how Jesus fulfilled every element of the old covenant, setting up something gloriously better. Hebrews 9 presents Jesus as the Great High Priest, who has ended the need for a temple priest to advocate to God on our behalf. Instead, Jesus is the greatest and highest priest of all, bridging the divide between God and us. Through His one-time death on the cross, Jesus gave the ultimate and final payment God required to restore humanity's relationship with Him. His sacrifice was applied to us, and through His blood, we now have direct access to God. No more priests, no more blood, no more six hundred laws. Just a relationship with Jesus.

Now **READ HEBREWS 10:1-18.** How would you summarize the purpose of the Law?

Why was it necessary for Jesus to die?

High Priest

The priest was in charge of the temple worship. Among his duties was overseeing the Day of Atonement, the one day a year when the high priest entered the holy of holies to atone for the sins of the nation (Leviticus 16).

The temple sacrifices would never be enough. There was always a need for more because there was always more sin in people's lives that needed forgiving. Yet, Jesus, the sinless sacrifice, died "once for all time" (10:10). He never sinned, but He took our place, dying the death we deserved.

Only God could reconcile us to Himself because we were stuck in our sin. Jesus bore the weight of it, experiencing death. Then, He rose again victorious over sin and death, ensuring there will be a day when both are no more. Jesus crossed the divide between God and man so that we would be reconciled to God. This happens when we put our trust in Christ. We die to sin and live unto Him!

If you are a follower of Jesus, then you are a child of God and a new creation "Therefore, if anyone is in Christ, he is a new creation; the old has passed away, and see, the new has come!" (2 Corinthians 5:17). Come to find out, I do want to be "washed in the blood of the Lamb" after all.

> As you consider the great humility and sacrifice of Jesus, ask yourself: To what lengths did God go to reconcile you to Himself?

> How does that encourage you to take on the same humility and obedience that Jesus exhibited?

Spend time in prayer thanking God for the phenomenal gift of Jesus who paid for your sin on the cross. Confess any sin that you have not repented of and ask for forgiveness and strength to walk in obedience, just as Jesus did.

FOR WHILE
WE WERE STILL
HELPLESS, AT
THE RIGHT TIME,
CHRIST DIED FOR
THE UNGODLY.

Romans 5:6

DAY
04

FREED
BY
FAITH

by Yana Jenay Conner

As people created in the image of God, justice matters to us. So when I think about things like an innocent person declared guilty or a guilty person left to roam free, I have a hard time deciding which is more egregious (*Both?*). One of the themes of the Bible is God's justice, and nowhere do we see that more clearly than at the cross, where our innocent Savior, Jesus Christ, is declared guilty so we, the guilty party, can be free.

This is the gospel message in a nutshell. What might seem egregious to us—this innocent for guilty transaction—is actually quite glorious. It's a beautiful picture of the heart of our God, the just Justifier.

This week we've been studying the transformation that happens when a person becomes a Christian—the incredible shift from death to life, broken to restored. We looked briefly at the book of Romans earlier in the week, and today we'll spend time studying Romans 3–5. But first, some context!

One of the reasons Paul wrote to the church in Rome was to ask them to help fund the cost of his trip to Spain as he traveled around telling people about Jesus (see Romans 15:22-24). But before getting to his request, Paul clearly and carefully explained the gospel message to them—the good news of Jesus's work on their behalf—and helped them understand how to live now that they were followers of Christ.

At the start of his letter, Paul described the gospel as "the power of God for salvation to everyone who believes, first to the Jew, and also to the Greek" (Romans 1:16). Paul used the term "Greek" here to refer to anyone who was not Jewish. Another term you might have heard is "Gentile." One of the earliest tensions among Christians centered on the conflict between Jewish Christians and Gentile (non-Jewish) Christians.

GENTILES

In general, the term "Gentile" refers to anyone who was not born part of God's covenant community, the Jews (Exodus 19). In the Old Testament, God chose, or set aside, the Jewish nation of Israel to live for Him and be a light for Him to the Gentile world (Isaiah 49:6). Then in the New Testament, Jesus came to be that light (Luke 2:32). Through His death and resurrection, Jews and Gentiles alike are invited into the family of God. The New Testament writers speak often in their letters about the oneness of Jews and Gentiles in the family of God (1 Peter 2:9-10).[10]

Abraham

Abraham's name means "father of a multitude." He was the first Hebrew patriarch who became known as the prime example of faith. His story is told in Genesis 11–25.[11]

Since the days of Abraham (see Genesis 12), the Jews had been the chosen people of God. This is the history of the Old Testament. That all changed with Jesus, but it seems from Paul's letter that some Jewish Christians wanted to hold on to their religious traditions and customs and continued to see themselves as favored in God's eyes.

In teaching extensively about the gospel, Paul leveled the playing field between Jews and Gentiles. In Romans 1:18-32, he presented evidence of the Gentiles' sin against God. In Romans 2:1–3:8, Paul presented evidence of the Jews' sin. In Romans 3:9-20, he made his closing arguments, deeming both parties guilty. He wrote:

> *⁹What then? Are we [the Jews] any better off? Not at all! For we have already charged that both Jews and Greeks [Gentiles] are all under sin, ¹⁰as it is written: There is no one righteous, not even one.*

ROMANS 3:9-10

While Paul's closing arguments concerning our sinful and guilty condition are true, God gives the final verdict. Let's read our just Justifier's ruling.

LOOK UP AND READ ROMANS 3:2-26. After you read, write verses 23-24 in the space below.

For even the most seasoned Christian this section of Paul's letter can be hard to wrap our minds around. But the heart of Paul's point is this: In Christ, God declares all who believe in Jesus, "Not guilty!" What amazing and undeserving grace! Despite our undeniable guilt—the sin nature we were born with—God freely wipes away our sin.

Since some key words in this passage aren't commonly used, let's consider their definitions.

- **RIGHTEOUSNESS** (Romans 3:21): To be in right relationship with God through faith in Christ.[12]

- **JUSTIFIED** (Romans 3:24): To be acquitted of guilty charges and declared innocent and righteous before God.[13]

- **ATONING SACRIFICE/PROPITIATION/MERCY SEAT** (Romans 3:25): Through His shed blood, Christ satisfied the wrath of God and makes it possible for the guilty to be acquitted, forgiven, and declared righteous.[14]

  With these definitions in mind, rewrite Romans 3:24 in your own words.

  Describe how God is both just and the One who justifies all who believe. (Hint: This is the good news of the gospel you've been studying!)

  God's gift of justification is a great cause for celebration. Fill in the blanks below in celebration of what Christ has done for you:

  In Christ, I am no longer _____ .

  In Christ, I am now _____ .

In Christ, we are no longer guilty sinners worthy of receiving God's wrath. Instead, because of Jesus and through relationship with Him, we are justified (made innocent), forgiven (made blameless), and righteous (made whole). God has displayed His perfect justice by presenting Christ as the sacrifice for the world's past, present, and future sins.

NOW READ ROMANS 4:1-8. What do you take away as Paul's primary point in this passage?

Though I have been walking with Jesus for twenty years, I still sometimes seek to earn favor or right standing with God through good works or behavior modification. However, my effort is futile and unfortunate, given the adequacy of Jesus's work on the cross. Only faith in Jesus makes me righteous. That is the point Paul drives home in Romans 4.

Are there ways you're currently seeking to earn favor or right standing with God? If so, how does Paul's teaching of faith as the only means for salvation challenge and/or comfort you?

NOW READ ROMANS 5:1-11, our final text for today.

In Romans 3:21-26, Paul answers the question: What is justification, and who does it come from? In Romans 4:1-8, he explains how a person receives this justification from God. Now, in Romans 5:1-11, he shares why it was given.

The gospel of God is amazing. God, our just Justifier, offers up His Son as an atoning sacrifice for sin so that guilty sinners, like you and me, can be declared righteous (justified) and be brought back into relationship with God. Through Jesus, we gain a relationship with our heavenly Father that is marked by peace, forgiveness, intimacy, and love.

Reflect on what you've learned today from Romans. What does God's desire for reconciliation reveal about His heart toward you?

Conclude your time in God's Word today by praying out loud to God, thanking and praising Him for His justifying grace.

DAY
05

ALIVE IN CHRIST

by Elizabeth Hyndman

I was listening to a trivia podcast recently where the four hosts were discussing Christianity and the Bible. Some of the four had a religious background, but at least one did not. He expressed shock over a miracle in Acts where Paul brought a man named Eutychus back to life (see Acts 20:7-12). As an explanation, the host who told the story said, "It's the Bible . . . That's the kind of thing that happens in the Bible." Another host replied, "Yeah. Zombies. Very common."[15]

The hosts were correct in that the Bible often talks about dead people rising up and walking again, but the idea of the walking dead couldn't be further from the truth. The Christian life is about the dead being made alive, and we see this in both spiritual and literal ways throughout the Bible. As you've read and studied the last few days, without Christ, you were dead in your sin; in Christ you are fully, abundantly alive (John 10:10).

> Look up the book of Ephesians, one of Paul's letters in the New Testament. Then **READ EPHESIANS 2:1-10.**

These verses are often cited as one of the most powerful pictures of the gospel in all of Scripture, and it all hinges on the "but God" transition of verse 4. Paul, the author of Ephesians, pointed out that all our befores looked similar—dead in our sin, walking according to the ways of the world, living in our fleshly desires.

> Think back to your English classes in school. What tense is employed in verses 1-3? Circle one:
>
> Past   Present   Future
>
> What about the end of verse 5? What tense does Paul arrive at? Circle one:
>
> Past   Present   Future

Everything before that famous "But God" is in past tense. That means "But God" makes it no longer true. You *were* dead; but now you *are* saved. Our befores were the same—dead. Our afters are also the same—alive! Now and forever.

THE LETTER TO THE EPHESIANS

Ephesians is the tenth book in the New Testament. "It is a letter attributed to the Apostle Paul and addressed to the Christians at Ephesus, a city on the western coast of Asia Minor (modern-day Turkey). Ephesians is one of four so-called Prison Letters (the others are Philippians, Colossians, and Philemon) and is commonly grouped with Colossians due to overlapping themes and structure. Ephesians might have been a circular letter sent to multiple churches in the region, including the congregation at Ephesus." You can read about Paul's time in Ephesus in Acts 19.[16]

Make side-by-side lists of the transformation described in Ephesians 2:1-10. On the left, note everything that was true about you apart from God. On the right, note who you are in Him.

BEFORE I WAS . . .	NOW I AM . . .

Now **REREAD EPHESIANS 2:8-10**. How was our salvation achieved? (Think back to what you studied in Day Four.)

I don't know about you, but it is a relief to me that I didn't have to earn my salvation. I couldn't. No amount of good works or charity donations or kindness toward people or volunteering could change my status from dead to alive. I needed a miracle. I needed grace.

Use a dictionary or look up the definition of *grace* online. Write it below.

Depending on which dictionary or search engine you used, you may have found definitions ranging from "a free gift of God to humankind for regeneration or sanctification"[17] to "simple elegance or refinement of movement."[18] While it does mean all of those things, for the purposes of this study, we're going to focus on the first definition.

We've seen how we deserved death, but instead God sent His Son to give us life. The grace of God is what makes this gift of life available. We've done nothing to deserve nor merit His love and forgiveness. It's purely a gift from God. Faith in Him is how we receive the gift. So that's what Ephesians 2:8 is saying—we are saved by grace through faith.

At this point in the study, you may be asking yourself, *Well, now what?* or *What does that mean for me on a daily basis?* Paul, in another of his letters, says, "Therefore, if anyone is in Christ, he is a new creation; the old has passed away, and see, the new has come!" (2 Corinthians 5:17). When we are saved by grace from death to life, we become new creations.

What do you think it means to be a new creation? What does that look like?

To be a new creation doesn't mean that we're starting over as actual, physical infants. But it does mean that our lives will look different. Remember Ephesians 2:1-3? It was all in past tense. Once we are saved by grace through faith, we are no longer dead in our sin. We no longer walk in the ways of the world or our fleshly desires. Now we walk in freedom and obedience to Christ. But we don't do this by ourselves or in our own power. We can't. We do so by the Holy Spirit who lives in us.

Does that mean that from the "But God" to eternity we will live sin-free lives? I wish that was the case! However, sadly, until we get to heaven we will continually struggle to put off sin. The difference is that now we do so as those who are already forgiven of those sins.

> Now turn to the book of Romans and **READ ROMANS 6:1-14**.
>
> These verses follow Paul's teaching on justification by grace through faith in Jesus, which we looked at yesterday. How would you summarize the main point of Romans 6:1-14?

A lot of people look at grace and the verses we've read and ask why we should even try to stay away from sin. Grace has us covered, right? Right. But, like these verses say, why would we want to keep living like dead people? We are not zombies! We are all the way alive in Christ.

In another of Paul's letters, he gives us a good description of what living life in this new way looks like: "But the fruit of the Spirit is love, joy, peace, patience, kindness, goodness, faithfulness, gentleness, and self-control" (Galatians 5:22-23). Those who are alive in Christ can experience and display peace, patience, love, joy, and on and on—the character of Christ.

> Verse 4 tells us to "walk in newness of life." How have you seen someone display and demonstrate "newness of life" in a practical way? How are you doing this?

What needs to change this week—a habit, an attitude, a thought, an action—for you to live like someone who is all the way alive in Christ?

Spend a few minutes in prayer, praising God for His grace that made you all the way alive. Ask Him to help you live like one who is walking not in sin, but in newness of life.

In the space below, on a separate piece of paper, or on your phone wallpaper, write out Ephesians 2:4-5. (It's included for you on page 10!) Try to commit these verses to memory over the next week.

REFLECT

Take a few minutes to reflect on the truths you uncovered in your study of God's Word this week. Journal any final thoughts below, or use the space to take notes during your Bible study group conversation. The three questions on the opposite page can be used for your personal reflection or group discussion.

_____

_____

_____

_____

_____

_____

_____

_____

_____

_____

_____

_____

_____

_____

_____

_____

_____

_____

_____

_____

Leading a group? Download the *Alive* leader guide at **lifeway.com/alive**.

As you reflect on the Bible passages you read this week, what stands out to you about the character of God?

How have you been challenged and encouraged in your relationship with Jesus through what you've learned?

Write down one way you can use what you've learned this week to encourage someone else.

Identity
WHO I AM

*But to all who did receive him, he gave them
the right to be children of God.*

JOHN 1:12

What does it mean to be a child of God, and how does that change my life? Will Jesus ever turn His back on me? What is the Holy Spirit's work in my life? What are spiritual gifts, and do I have any? In this week of study, you'll consider these questions and more to help you better understand who you are in Christ and explore the benefits and blessings that come with being a child of God.

DAY 01

I AM A CHILD OF GOD

by Blair Linne

The Bible often uses the child-parent relationship to describe the relationship believers have with God. Think about the relationship (or lack thereof) you have with your earthly parents. For better or worse, the people who raised us influenced us. We mimic mannerisms and behaviors, share habits and quirks, and are heavily influenced by genetics, heritage, and customs. Through imitation, we show whose children we are.

Our relationship with our heavenly Father is one of influence and imitation, too. Today we'll consider what it means to be a child of God and how we're forever transformed by our relationship with Him.

The Gospels

The Gospels are the first four books of the New Testament— Matthew, Mark, Luke, and John. The term gospel *comes from a Greek word meaning "good news."*

> Find the Gospel of John (the fourth book of the New Testament) and **READ JOHN 1:1-14.** Then reread verses 12-13, printed here.
>
> *¹²But to all who did receive him, he gave them the right to be children of God, to those who believe in his name, ¹³who were born, not of natural descent, or of the will of the flesh, or of the will of man, but of God.*

Early on in his Gospel, John—the beloved disciple (follower) of Jesus (John 13:23)—describes how we can be certain that we are children of God. But before we get there, we must clear away any false ideas that we have. John is quick to point out that being a child of God is not based on heritage or ancestry; it's not based on desire or interest ("the will of flesh"); and it's not based on personal determination ("the will of man"). John's point is clear: A relationship with God is not the result of anything a person does on her own apart from God.

> Have you ever believed that you could become God's child through ancestry (such as having Christian parents or mentors), having an emotional moment with God (fleshly desire), or through your own will (or determination)? Where did that belief lead you?

So then, how do we become children of God? **REREAD JOHN 1:12** and think back to what you learned in the previous week of study, then note any thoughts you have. (Hint: Focus on the verbs in the verse!)

John highlights two verbs in verse 12 that help us understand God's work in our lives—"receive" and "believe."

RECEIVE

First, John says the child of God is the person who has "received him." Based on John 1:1-14, we know the "him" here is Jesus, the Word who became flesh (John 1:14). *Receive* means "to take possession of," or "welcome."[1] Rather than respond like Jesus's own people who rejected Him (John 1:10-11), the child of God is the one who receives Him, the one who embraces who He is and what He wants to do in one's life.

In just the first chapter of John alone, the disciple opens our eyes to who Jesus is. Before we can receive Jesus, we have to know who He is. Unveiling this is the goal of the Gospels. John emphasizes Jesus as the divine Prophet, Priest, and King who gives His own blood to save sinners and make them children of the Father.

Read the following verses. Below each verse, note anything you learn about receiving things from God.

John responded, "No one can receive anything unless it has been given to him from heaven."

JOHN 3:27

Jesus is . . .

The Word (1:1-2)

The Creator (1:3)

The Word who became flesh (1:14)

Eternal Life (1:9; 3:16)

The Lamb of God (1:29,36)

The true light (1:5,9)

The One who baptizes with the Holy Spirit (1:33)

The Son of God (1:18,34,49)

The Messiah (1:41)

King of Israel (1:49)

Son of Man (1:51)

But the person without the Spirit does not receive what comes from God's Spirit, because it is foolishness to him; he is not able to understand it since it is evaluated spiritually.

1 CORINTHIANS 2:14

For you did not receive a spirit of slavery to fall back into fear. Instead, you received the Spirit of adoption, by whom we cry out, "Abba, Father!"

ROMANS 8:15

Receiving Jesus means we need a spiritual awakening from above, which we receive through the power of the Holy Spirit at work in us. God's Spirit opens our eyes to see Jesus for who He is, just like He opened John the Baptist's eyes to recognize Jesus from among everyone else (John 1:32-34). Once we see that Jesus is the sufficient Lamb of God (1:19), we receive Him by faith.

BELIEVE

Second, John says we are to "believe in his name" (John 1:12).

Look up *believe* in a dictionary and write the definition here.

With that definition in mind, what do you think it means to believe in the name of Jesus?

Believe is defined as "accept[ing] something as true, genuine, or real; to have a firm conviction as to the goodness, efficacy, or ability of something."[2] One's name refers to their authority, character, or rank. Because He is the divine Word, the Son of God, Jesus's name is filled with power and authority (see John 5:43). So, to believe in the name of Jesus means to accept He is who He says He is—God's own Son, who lived, died, and rose again to save us from our sins.

Everything changes relationally between us and God when we personally receive Christ and believe in Him.

Now that we are God's children it means He is our Father. Imagine our prayers being like the cries of a newborn baby who trusts her parent to supply her needs and nourish her body as she grows and matures. As we grow up in Christ, we shed anything related to the former life that is not pleasing to God while being renewed in our spirit so that we look more and more like our Father. This is how we learn to imitate Him, and it's a process we never stop.

> Now look up and **READ ROMANS 8:1-17**, focusing closely
> on verses 14-17. Note one or two observations you have from
> verses 14-17 about what it means to be a child of God.

God only has one begotten Son, and His name is Jesus (John 3:16). However, Jesus was not ashamed to call the sons of Adam (us) brothers. The Son of God voluntarily identified with us to exchange the wrath our sin deserved for the welcome His righteousness affords. Paul says in Romans 8:14-17 that we can call God our Father now, since Jesus grants us access to His Father through adoption.

Paul highlights some of the specific privileges we have as adopted children of God, and they are life-altering:

- The security of being a child of God (Romans 8:14-15).

- The ability to intimately cry out to God and be heard (Romans 8:15-16).

- The Holy Spirit in us who testifies we belong to God (Romans 8:16).

- Our shared inheritance in the promises of God, including the promise of a glorious future with God (Romans 8:17).

Adoption means becoming a part of the divine family of God both now and forever. This means that we share everything, from our temporary suffering to our future in heaven, with Jesus. We have a beautiful inheritance awaiting us as coheirs with Christ; this world is not our home. When we experience glorification upon our Lord's return, we will receive our promised inheritance, reserved for all the children of God (1 Peter 1:4).

Reflect on what you've read today. As you think about your identity as a child of God and coheir with Christ, what is the dominant emotion you are feeling?

What are two areas where you need to ask God to help you imitate Him?

Spend a few minutes in prayer, thanking God for revealing the truth of who Jesus is to you and for embracing you as His beloved daughter.

DAY
02

I AM
KNOWN

by Blair Linne

The difference between being "known" by others and really, truly being known is nowhere more evident than on social media platforms. People often feel much more isolated and much less known than we may realize. The difference between knowing people and being known highlights a type of knowledge from God we read about in Scripture.

God is omniscient, which means He possesses complete knowledge of the past, present, and future, a level of knowledge so precise that it's hard for us to wrap our minds around (1 John 3:20). However, Psalm 138:6 says that God "knows the haughty from a distance." Also, Jesus says in Matthew 7:22-23, "On that day, many will say to me, 'Lord, Lord,' . . . then I will announce to them, 'I never knew you. Depart from me.'" One might read that and think, *But I thought God knew everything and everybody!* I assure you, He does. However, Scripture makes a distinction between those God knows because He created them and those God has a relationship with (those who are His children).

For the follower of Christ, the Bible is clear that God knows us well and is with us always. Jesus said, "I am the good shepherd. I know my own, and my own know me, just as the Father knows me, and I know the Father. I lay down my life for the sheep" (John 10:14-15). Jesus's death and resurrection made a relationship with God possible for you, His sheep. Let's consider why this is such good news.

> **READ PSALM 139.** Pick one verse related to God's knowledge of you, and write it here.

God knows the psalmist well; that is clear from verse 1. The psalmist (who we know from the psalm's heading is King David) starts off saying, "LORD, you have searched me and known me." God knows the details of our lives from beginning to end, and He is intimately acquainted with all our ways. David highlighted several ways this shows up in a person's relationship with God, and I want to draw your attention to three of them—God knows your frame, your heart, and your spirit.

King David

The first king to unite Israel and Judah and the first to receive the promise of a royal Messiah in his line. He is believed to have written more than seventy of the psalms.[3]

THE BOOK OF PSALMS

Found in the middle of the Bible, the Old Testament book of Psalms is a collection of songs, poems, and prayers to God. The 150 psalms in this book "are written from the human perspective as authors work their way through various life situations. The struggle to understand how God's attributes, particularly his sovereignty and goodness, relate to life experiences is a major theme in the collection. These words are from people who had not lost their faith in God, although they might have been tempted to at times (Psalm 73). They wrestled with how God was dealing with them personally and as a community."[4]

GOD KNOWS YOUR FRAME.

> **READ PSALM 139:13-16.** Summarize how David viewed God's creation of his body.

As the Creator of all things, God is the one who made you, and He didn't do so haphazardly. David's poetic statements in verses 13-16 speak to God's detailed involvement in creating each of His children. God is your Designer, and He has compiled each circumstance to make you exactly who you're supposed to be. God even planned your personality—every attribute that makes you unique. Whether you prefer one-on-one interaction or can entertain a crowd, whether you're soft spoken or have a big belly laugh, whether your hair is black or red or gray; God crafted you with intentionality and purpose.

GOD KNOWS YOUR HEART.

At several points in Psalm 139, David comments on how God knows his heart—his inward desires and the depths of who he really is. Did you know God has this knowledge of you? God knows the thoughts that no one else hears, whether good or bad (v. 2). He sees the compassion and love that you have toward Christians, strangers, and even "enemies." God knows how you seek to love what He loves and hate what He hates (vv. 19-22). He also sees when you feel blah and are weary of the fallenness of the world. He sees the jealous thoughts when you compare what others possess to what you do not, the unforgiving thoughts swirling around that tell you to show no mercy, the fear-filled thoughts that paralyze you from trusting God wholeheartedly. He is familiar with all your inward ways. He knows the source of every word spoken, whether it be fear or trust (v. 4). The depth of who we are in all our sinfulness—not who we want people to think we are—is exposed before Him. God knows all of this about you, and yet, He draws you close to Himself (v. 5).

> **REREAD PSALM 139:5-6.** Then write your own paraphrase of these verses.

GOD KNOWS YOUR SPIRIT.

In Psalm 139:7, David asks two rhetorical questions: "Where can I go to escape your Spirit? Where can I flee from your presence?" Of course, the answer is nowhere. God is present everywhere, including with the Christian forever (vv. 8-10). He is aware of your human limits—He knows when you in weakness must sit, or when you have strength to stand (v. 2), when in vigor we travel to different places, or when we need to rest because we're tired and weary (v. 3). No darkness will keep you from Him because the light of His presence will find you (vv. 11-12). Every day, the ups and downs, the triumphs and trials, are used in God's good plan for you. You can trust that God will sustain you spiritually no matter where you find yourself.

> **READ VERSES 23-24.** What would it look like for you to lean into God's knowledge of your spirit like David did? What hinders you from bringing your complete self to God?

Omnipresence

The character trait of God that means He is present everywhere, all the time.

Notice how David isn't afraid to be known by God. God's omniscience doesn't produce anxiety in him; rather he praises God for knowing him (v. 14) and in faith trusts that if there is any part of him that is offensive or sinful, God will give the ability to turn away and turn to God (v. 24). The fact that God has complete knowledge is a great comfort to him, as it should be for us.

Take a moment to reflect on the things God knows about you. Next to each category below, write a few thoughts about what it means to you that God knows you in that way.

GOD KNOWS YOUR FRAME	
GOD KNOWS YOUR HEART	
GOD KNOWS YOUR SPIRIT	

Our connection to Jesus as His sheep makes all the difference in us being known by God. Our faithful Shepherd will carry us all the way home, while fully aware of our frame, our heart, and our spirit. There is no need to hide from the God who knows and sees all. No circumstance is too easy or difficult to try to work out on our own. Our God knows us. May our response always be, "I will praise you because I have been remarkably and wondrously made" (Psalm 139:14).

Take time now to praise God, using the characteristics and actions that describe Him in Psalm 139 as a guide for your prayer.

LORD, YOU HAVE
SEARCHED ME
AND KNOWN ME.
YOU KNOW WHEN
I SIT DOWN AND
WHEN I STAND UP;
YOU UNDERSTAND
MY THOUGHTS
FROM FAR AWAY.

Psalm 139:1-2

DAY 03

I AM
EMPOWERED

by Christine Thornton

Last week, you learned that as a Christian you are alive in Christ. When Jesus died, was buried, and rose to new life, you died, were buried, and were raised to new life in Him. But this leads to other questions like, "How?" and, "So what?" How does the life, death, and resurrection of Jesus become my life, death, and resurrection? And what does this mean for my life as a Christian?

Thankfully, these questions have answers, and the Bible connects the dots for us. Christ's life becomes our life by the power of His Holy Spirit. Christians live in Christ by the power of the Spirit and, through Him, grow up to be mature.

When we desire to learn about the role of the Holy Spirit in our ongoing Christian life, we always begin with the gospel of the Lord Jesus Christ. From there, we can understand the ongoing work of the Spirit in relation to the Jesus we know and love.

> Read the following Bible verses, and (circle) each mention of the Holy Spirit.

16 When Jesus was baptized, he went up immediately from the water. The heavens suddenly opened for him, and he saw the Spirit of God descending like a dove and coming down on him. 17 And a voice from heaven said, "This is my beloved Son, with whom I am well-pleased."

MATTHEW 3:16-17

Nevertheless, I am telling you the truth. It is for your benefit that I go away, because if I don't go away the Counselor will not come to you. If I go, I will send him to you.

JOHN 16:7

Therefore, since he has been exalted to the right hand of God and has received from the Father the promised Holy Spirit, he has poured out what you both see and hear.

ACTS 2:33

From these verses, what can you conclude is the relationship between Jesus Christ (the Son of God) and the Holy Spirit?

Holy Spirit

The Holy Spirit is "the third Person of the Trinity through whom God acts, reveals His will, empowers individuals, and discloses His personal presence in the Old and New Testament."[5]

In order to know how we live empowered by the Holy Spirit, we must first understand who He is. We don't have time for a full Trinity lesson here, but in each of these verses we see that there's a Trinitarian chain that reaches down to us in order to save and equip us. Jesus, the Son, receives the Spirit from the Father (like in Matthew 3:16-17 and Acts 2:33). When Jesus is exalted or goes away (John 16:7) after the resurrection, He pours the Holy Spirit out on His followers, which empowers them for holy living and mission. God has given us Himself by sending the Holy Spirit to empower us, and the Holy Spirit is one and the same with the Father and the Son.

Take a minute to reflect on the fact that God has given Himself to us in the Spirit. How does this strengthen your faith in Him?

LOOK UP AND READ ROMANS 8:9-11. What role does the Holy Spirit play in our salvation?

Not only did Christ die and rise through the power of the Holy Spirit, but we also died and rose with Him by means of that same Spirit. Notice that in verse 9 Paul says, "The Spirit of God lives in you," and then in verse 10 He says, "Christ is in you." In other words, when the Spirit lives in you, Christ Himself lives in you. If Christ lives in you by His Spirit, then when He died you died, and when He came back to life, you received new life (Romans 8:10). Through the power of the Spirit, we are united to Christ.

We are already, and finally, raised to new life in Christ by the power of the Spirit.

Had you considered that the indwelling of the Spirit unites you to Christ? How does this reality encourage your faith in God?

Now look up and read the following passages, which give us our "So what?" Next to each reference, record what you learn about the role the Holy Spirit plays in the life of a Christian.

ROMANS 8:11-12	
GALATIANS 3:1-6	
GALATIANS 5:16-26	

Because you have already been raised to new life in Christ by the Spirit, now you can live like who you already are. You are no longer trapped in sin (or "obligated to the flesh," Romans 8:12). You are free and empowered to live your life in the likeness of Jesus (lovingly, humbly, and selflessly, for starters).

This idea feels foreign to many of us for one of two reasons. Sometimes we feel like in order to live a holy life, we have to rely on our own effort. This view stands in opposition to the gospel. You can only continue in Christ the way you began—in the Spirit (Galatians 3:3). Other times we feel like there's no way we can actually live in Christlikeness. This also opposes the gospel because those who belong to Christ have already "crucified the flesh with its passions and desires" (Galatians 5:24). Because you are already alive by the Spirit, you can keep in step with Him (Galatians 5:25).

As a Christian, the very power of God lives in you and has raised you to new life in Christ. As surely as you are now alive in Him, you are empowered to live life like Christ. So, on days when holy living feels impossible, remember that the power you need doesn't come from you. It comes from the Spirit of Christ, who is already yours. In Him, you have all the power you need.

Take a minute to remember the gospel. As you reflect on the life, death, and resurrection of Jesus, ask God to help you actively remember that you have already died in Christ and are risen in Him.

DAY
04

I AM
SECURE

by Christine Thornton

How can I know that I'm really saved? Can I lose my salvation?

Questions like these arise in the hearts of all Christians at one point or another. The anxious moments when our hearts begin to wonder can conjure a fear that pierces us to the core. But the gospel that changed our lives is still good news that can calm our restless hearts. We were saved by God's grace and we are kept by God's grace. As surely as Jesus has died and is risen, we are safe, and we are saved. We are secure in Him.

In addition to the Gospel of John, the apostle John wrote three letters included in the New Testament. In his first letter, he presents a series of direct statements about who is a Christian and who isn't. At multiple points in the letter, he addresses the deep longing of Christian hearts to know we are really saved. In today's study, we'll walk through two key passages from 1 John about the assurance we have in Christ and the simplicity of our perseverance in him.

> **READ 1 JOHN 1:5-10.** What do these verses teach us about when Christians sin? See if you can pinpoint two key points.

1, 2, 3 John

John's letters are found toward the end of the New Testament, just before Jude and Revelation. All three share overlapping themes with John's Gospel.

First, we learn that "the blood of Jesus his Son cleanses us from all sin" (v. 7). There is no sin too great that it can't be cleansed by the blood of Jesus. It doesn't matter whether those sins were committed before or after becoming a Christian. The blood of Christ covers all. The blood that saved you is powerful enough to keep you.

Second, God is "faithful and just" to forgive our sin and "cleanse us from all unrighteousness" when we confess (v. 9). Now, the need for confession isn't a requirement. John is not saying you have to confess your sins (all the ways you've failed God) and name them one-by-one or you are still accountable for them. Rather, when we put all the pieces of the passage together, we see that those who are in Christ live in humility and faith. We acknowledge both our sin before God (vv. 8,10) and that Jesus has cleansed that sin (vv. 7,9). Confession becomes what you naturally do when you have this disposition of humble faith in Christ. We confess our sins as the natural overflow of our faith in Christ, and this confession instills confidence that He has forgiven all our sin.

After you are made alive in Christ, there is no sin that can soil the purity you have in Him. It can't be undone. Ever.

READ BACK OVER 1 JOHN 1:5-10, THEN TAKE A MOMENT TO PRACTICE CONFESSION. Voice your sorrow over any sins to God, then receive His forgiveness. As part of your prayer, praise Him for His grace and love.

NOW READ 1 JOHN 3:19-24. Next to each verse number below, write down any phrases that can reassure you of your salvation.

VERSE 20	
VERSES 21-22	
VERSE 23	

If you ever question how secure you are in Christ, come back to these verses. They are full of reassurances that nothing can separate you from His love. First, we read that God is greater than the doubts of our hearts (3:20). Not even your doubting can make you lose your salvation because God is greater than even your doubts. Trust Him more than you trust yourself.

Second, we can "have confidence before God . . . because we keep his commands" (3:21-22). Wait a minute—does this mean our obedience to God is what keeps us secure in Him? If we stopped at verse 22, it definitely would seem that John was encouraging us to reassure our hearts according to our own good works—which isn't actually very reassuring at all. We know all too well the depth of our own shortcomings to obey God's law. The law can never give us confidence before God—only the awareness of our inability to keep it. Faith in our own obedience never brings assurance. It only exacerbates our insecurities.

So, what command do we keep that gives us confidence before God? "We believe in the name of his Son, Jesus Christ" (3:23). The command isn't to live a life of legalism, governed by our long to-do list of right and wrong. The command is simply to believe in Jesus. We never approach God on the basis of our own good works. We have confidence before God by faith in Christ alone. Jesus Christ gives us confidence and assurance.

We are kept safe in the very same way that we were saved at first—by believing in Jesus. It's really that simple.

So, how can we be assured that we can't lose our salvation? Because the gospel is as true today as it was when you first believed. Any attempt to calm our hearts that begins with "I am saved because I . . ." will always end in disastrous angst. We must begin with "I am saved because Jesus . . ." Only the reminder of who Jesus is and what He has done can quiet our hearts and give us lasting assurance.

Legalism

The emphasis "on obedience to laws or moral codes based on the assumption that such obedience is a means of gaining divine favor."[6]

As we finish today's study, make your own list of "I am saved because Jesus . . ." statements to rehearse the gospel and encourage your faith in Him.

Here are a few examples to get you started:

I am saved **because Jesus loves me.**

I am saved **because Jesus is faithful and just to forgive me.**

I am saved **because Jesus died in my place.**

I am saved **because Jesus is risen from the dead, and I rose with Him.**

Now make your own list!

DAY
05

I AM
GIFTED

by Ashley Marivittori Gorman

Niccolò Paganini was a world-renowned Italian violinist, composer, and showman in the 1800s who forever changed violin technique. Upon his death, he willed his beloved and beautiful violin to the city of Genoa as a gift. Paganini's will had one condition in order for the city to receive his famous violin: that it be outfitted for "perpetual conservation"—that no one ever play the instrument, or if they must, it be done sparingly. At first the city of Genoa abided by these conditions strictly, but as time passed, it became clear that certain kinds of wood need to be regularly handled to prevent decay. If this gift was going to last, then it had to be used. Today, the city of Genoa keeps this famous violin in a museum and allows the violin to be unsealed from its case and played by an expert once a year to help it stand the test of time.[7]

Throughout his New Testament letters, the apostle Paul teaches us that while we are each individual children of God, we are not isolated and autonomous. Rather, we are part of a larger body of Christians known as the church. Each of us serves a unique function that contributes to the whole. While there are many ways each individual person within the church differs from another, Paul narrows in on one major way each member is unique: his or her spiritual gifts. The tale of Paganini's violin helps us understand how our spiritual gifts, which we'll learn more about today, are at their best when they are actually used in service to others.

> Read the following passages from Paul's letters. We'll refer back to these passages throughout today's study. As you read, circle each example of spiritual gifts you find.

⁴Now as we have many parts in one body, and all the parts do not have the same function, ⁵in the same way we who are many are one body in Christ and individually members of one another. ⁶According to the grace given to us, we have different gifts: If prophecy, use it according to the proportion of one's faith; ⁷if service, use it in service; if teaching, in teaching; ⁸if exhorting, in exhortation; giving, with generosity; leading, with diligence; showing mercy, with cheerfulness.

ROMANS 12:4-8

⁴Now there are different gifts, but the same Spirit. ⁵There are different ministries, but the same Lord. ⁶And there are different activities, but the same God works all of them in each person. ⁷A manifestation of the Spirit is given to each person for the common good: ⁸to one is given a message of wisdom through the Spirit, to another, a message of knowledge by the same Spirit, ⁹to another, faith by the same Spirit, to another, gifts of healing by the one Spirit, ¹⁰to another, the performing of miracles, to another, prophecy, to another, distinguishing between spirits, to another, different kinds of tongues, to another, interpretation of tongues.

1 CORINTHIANS 12:4-10

[11]And he himself gave some to be apostles, some prophets, some evangelists, some pastors and teachers, [12]to equip the saints for the work of ministry, to build up the body of Christ.

EPHESIANS 4:11-12

[10]Just as each one has received a gift, use it to serve others, as good stewards of the varied grace of God. [11]If anyone speaks, let it be as one who speaks God's words; if anyone serves, let it be from the strength God provides, so that God may be glorified through Jesus Christ in everything. To him be the glory and the power forever and ever. Amen.

1 PETER 4:10-11

In these passages, we see various lists of spiritual gifts—one or more of which you yourself may possess! In New Testament lists like these, Paul is not offering a comprehensive catalog for us to choose from; he is giving various examples of what spiritual gifts can look like when at work in the greater body.[8]

TYPES OF GIFTS

Many Christian thinkers organize these gifts in broad categories based on the three offices that Jesus Christ Himself fulfilled: prophet, priest, and king.[9] Prophetic gifts display a person's ability to understand and articulate truth. Priestly gifts display a person's ability to notice and supply the basic needs of others. Kingly gifts display a person's ability to direct and lead a group based on its needs, having the faith to envision a goal clearly and move a gathering toward the goal. Still other Christian thinkers prefer to categorize the gifts in two major groups: gifts of speaking and gifts of service.[10]

Christians today disagree whether all of these gifts are still active. Some believe all the spiritual gifts are, while others believe that the miraculous gifts (sometimes called "sign" gifts)—including healing, miracles, and tongues—are no longer active today, as these gifts were God's temporary way of verifying His revelation until the Bible was composed and finalized. Regardless of which position you take, rest assured that there are faithful, biblically sound Christians who land on both sides of the discussion.

REREAD 1 CORINTHIANS 12:7. To whom are spiritual gifts given?

Notice one of the most encouraging things about spiritual gifts in these verses: they are not given to a select group of elite Christians. They are not given to some of us, or even most of us. They are given to "each of us"! To each person in the church. Every believer—including you!—has at least one God-given gift to share with others.

God's Word also reminds us that our spiritual gift was never something we manufactured or mustered up on our own. Our gift was something "given" to us (Romans 12:6); something that we "received" (1 Peter 4:10) depending on the will and distribution of the Holy Spirit (1 Corinthians 12:11); something originally belonging to someone else that we "steward" as a manager, not something that originated from ourselves (1 Peter 4:10). This truth should be so freeing: the pressure is not on you to be the source of your gift; you are simply the steward of the gift(s) God has given you.

> From the verses you've read, summarize in your own words the purpose of all spiritual gifts. Pay close attention to 1 Corinthians 12:7, 1 Peter 4:10, and Ephesians 4:12.

While it may be tempting to think that your gift is given to you simply to make you unique and special, Scripture tells us that the true purpose of any spiritual gift isn't you-oriented at all. It's others-oriented. The point of your gift is to build up others in the church. When you don't show up and exercise your gift among God's people, they miss out. They need the gifts God has given you, and you need the gifts God has given them.

So, next time you enter your community of faith, resist the temptation to ask how you might stand out because of your gift. Instead, ask who might need your gift right now, given what they are going through. Remember: the reason you are gifted is for someone else, and exercising your gift gives them the chance to benefit in their time of need. Your spiritual gift is a lot like Paganini's violin. It isn't meant to be hoarded or stored away. Rather, it is at its best when it's used in service to others. Take the time to discover the gift God has given you and find ways to exercise it— God will be glorified, and the church will end up better and stronger!

As you wrap up your study today, spend time in prayer, asking God to give you clarity as you consider how He has gifted you to serve Him and His church.

 ## DISCOVERING YOUR GIFTS

All this talk of gifts probably has you wondering what your spiritual gifts are. While there are online tests you can take, a helpful rule of thumb is to find the intersection point between these areas:

- An area of ministry or a calling you feel constantly burdened about (What issue can you not get off your mind?)

- An area of obvious need in your church (Where does your church have a ministry hole to fill?)

- An area of strength in the way God has made you (What are you good at?)

- An area of your life that Christian community has been consistently affirming in you (What have other Christians confirmed as a strength?)

Curious to learn more about your spiritual gifts? Take the spiritual gift inventory available as a free download on lifeway.com/alive.

IN THE SAME WAY
WE WHO ARE MANY
ARE ONE BODY
IN CHRIST AND
INDIVIDUALLY
MEMBERS OF
ONE ANOTHER.

Romans 12:5

REFLECT

Take a few minutes to reflect on the truths you uncovered in your study of God's Word this week. Journal any final thoughts below, or use the space to take notes during your Bible study group conversation. The three questions on the opposite page can be used for your personal reflection or group discussion.

_____

_____

_____

_____

_____

_____

_____

_____

_____

_____

_____

_____

_____

_____

_____

_____

_____

_____

_____

_____

Leading a group? Download the _Alive_ leader guide at **lifeway.com/alive**.

As you reflect on the Bible passages you read this week, what stands out to you about the character of God?

How have you been challenged and encouraged in your relationship with Jesus through what you've learned?

Write down one way you can use what you've learned this week to encourage someone else.

Community
LIFE
TOGETHER

And let us consider one another in order
to provoke love and good works.

HEBREWS 10:24

One of the most beautiful aspects of the Christian life is that relationships matter. Our faith is to be lived out in community, which means we don't have to do this alone. This week we'll explore some of the different facets of life together in the body of Christ—things like the value of the local church, why baptism and the Lord's Supper are important, why we gather together for worship, and our responsibilities in and to the family of God.

DAY 01

WE ARE THE CHURCH

by Ashley Marivittori Gorman

Last week we enjoyed discovering who we are, individually, in Christ. But there's more! Life in Christ has a communal component, too. In other words, when it comes to the Christian life, you're not just a "me;" you're part of a "we"—the church.

LET'S BEGIN BY READING 1 CORINTHIANS 12:12-27.

What analogy did Paul use to describe the church? (Hint: Look at verse 12.) Why is this analogy fitting?

As you read through verses 12-27, note how many times the word *one* is used. _____

Next, read through the verses again, and note how many times the word *many* is used. _____

What big idea do you think Paul is trying to communicate by repeating these two concepts?

🔖 *FIRST CORINTHIANS*

The New Testament letters of 1 and 2 Corinthians appear early in the New Testament, following the Gospels, Acts, and Romans. Both letters were written by the apostle Paul to the Corinthian church. Paul's time in Corinth is recorded in Acts 18. Paul's purpose in writing 1 Corinthians was to motivate the Corinthian church to acknowledge the Lord's ownership of them and the implications this had in their lives. Key topics Paul addressed in this overarching theme of the ownership and authority of the Lord include: Christian unity, morality, the role of women, spiritual gifts, and the resurrection.[1]

As many Christian thinkers will point out, the church is not a place, it's a people. God's people! And the Bible is filled with many word pictures and analogies to help us understand the nature and purpose of God's people. Here are just a few:

A PHYSICAL BODY—Ephesians 4:11-16; Colossians 1:18,24

A BRIDE—Isaiah 62:5; Matthew 25:1-13; Revelation 21:2-9

A HOUSEHOLD—Galatians 6:10; Ephesians 2:19; 1 Timothy 3:15

A TEMPLE—Ephesians 2:19-22; 1 Corinthians 3:16-17; Revelation 3:12

A FLOCK—Psalm 23; John 10:11-16; John 21:15-17; Acts 20:28-29; 1 Peter 5:2-4

A common theme is obvious in each of these—many individual parts that combine to make up one corporate whole. It may be easier to think of yourself only as an individual in your journey with Christ, but the Bible is clear in each of these pictures of the church: You don't just belong to Christ on a solo level, you belong to His people. Along with other Christians, you now have a shared identity as brothers and sisters in the family of God the Father and Christ the Son, joined together by the binding love of the Holy Spirit. Uniting your life to Christ means uniting your life to the rest of the members, stones, and sheep who have been rescued by Him too!

> Why do you think it's so easy to view a relationship with Jesus as a "solo" thing instead of a communal thing? What are some things we risk losing if we don't embrace our shared identity with other believers?

Being one part of a whole group comes with a sense of safety and belonging, but it can come with struggles too. **REREAD 1 CORINTHIANS 12:15-24.**

As verses 15-24 show us, one of the struggles in the church is when members compare one another instead of focusing on building one another up. Struggling with comparison can take the form of two pitfalls. One is underestimating (or even dismissing) your contribution to the greater church because you think other members are more influential, talented, or important compared to you. The other pitfall is the opposite problem: overestimating your part to play in the greater church because you think other members are less influential, talented, or important compared to you. Thankfully, 1 Corinthians 12 reveals that those in either pitfall need to hear the same thing: having a complete body of Christ requires all the parts to show up!

What is a practical step you need to take to either take your place among God's people, or make room for others?

THE GLOBAL CHURCH AND THE LOCAL CHURCH

When you become a Christian, you become a member of the global church—all Christians everywhere who make up God's great heavenly assembly. This would include all Christians who have come before you, all current Christians, and all Christians who will come after you. But it's also important that you become a member of a local church. Consider the book of 1 Corinthians, when Paul repeats the phrase "when you come together" (or in other translations, "when you assemble") six different times. Paul assumes these Corinthian Christians are assembling to worship together often in their city. While there are some understandable reasons a Christian may not be able to attend their local church gathering every now and then (illness, travel, etc.), it is clear that the Bible assumes that a Christian is not only a member of the greater global church, but an involved member of a local church that consistently gathers in person.

NOW TURN BACK TO THE BOOK OF ACTS AND READ ACTS 2:22-47.

These verses describe the very origin of the church following Jesus's earthly ministry and His sending of the Holy Spirit in His place. Here Peter is living out the Great Commission (Matthew 28:19-20) by preaching the good news of the gospel—the death and resurrection of Jesus the Messiah. People responded to the gospel by repenting of their sins, being baptized, and joining this body of believers.

In the description of this early church found in verse 42,
what did the believers devote their time and attention to?

What was the result of the early church functioning
in healthy ways?

While we know the local church is important, the question remains: what should
a local church be doing, exactly? Thankfully, in Acts 2, we are given a picture of
the early church and we can observe what it prioritized during its time together.
In Acts 2:42, first we see the priority of the "apostles' teaching." The teaching of
a church is of primary importance. A healthy church will align with Scripture no
matter what, and it will be gospel-centered in the way it leads its members.

Next, we see the early church was committed to "fellowship" and to "the
breaking of bread" and to "prayer." This means that a healthy local church
should be regularly *meeting together*, regularly *practicing ordinances* like the
Lord's Supper and baptism (more on this in the next two days of study), and
praying with one another consistently.

In verses 44-45, these believers display financial care and concern for each other,
even to the point of selling their possessions in order to provide the needs of other
church members. Here we learn another priority for a church: *generosity*. We can
also see two other priorities in verse 47: "praising God and enjoying the favor of
all the people." From this (along with many other passages in the Bible) we can
conclude that dedicated time to *praise God in worship* is a priority when a church
assembles, along with a generally respectable reputation throughout the city where
the church is planted.

And finally, in verse 47, we see that the Lord was adding to the number of this
early church. From this we can conclude that a healthy local church should be a
beacon of light to the watching world, revealing the unmatchable value of Jesus and
inspiring unbelievers to join Christ and His church by the strength of the Lord's
drawing power.

What are some excuses you've used or heard for neglecting to be a consistent member of a local church?

What may be holding you back from fully participating in a local church?

Now that you know you're part of a "we" and not just a "me," how can you better explore your new shared identity in Christ? Join a local church, or invest more if you already have one! There's no better way to take your place in the greater whole than getting around other believers in your church. You can do this by serving on a volunteer team, joining a small group or Bible study, signing up for enrichment classes, beginning a mentor relationship with a mature believer who can help you grow, attending prayer meetings, or participating in your church's local outreach initiatives.

In all these ways and more, you'll get to know your shared identity as a part of God's people. As a bonus, you'll get to know yourself better too, as who you are always comes into sharper focus when you're participating in community.

Spend time praising God for the church. Praise Him for being a God who delights in relationships and who understands our need for one another.

DAY 02

WE ARE BAPTIZED WITH CHRIST

by Tina Boesch

When I was growing up our family lived near the beach, so I spent many summer days at the shore. I'll never forget one particular day at the ocean after a storm swept through. I fearlessly dove in to play in the waves but wasn't prepared for the relentless undertow. At first, I felt confident jumping the small waves and diving through the towering ones, but suddenly and unexpectedly my strength failed. I couldn't keep my head above water. I couldn't breathe. A watery grave felt imminent.

Reliving the fear that I felt that day helps me understand part of the imagery of baptism in a more powerful way. Before starting a new life in Christ, we have to die with Him. The motion of falling back into the water during baptism is an image of our surrender to death and burial with Jesus as our old lives are washed away.

BAPTISM

Baptism refers to "the immersion or dipping of a believer in water symbolizing the complete renewal and change in the believer's life and testifying to the death, burial, and resurrection of Jesus Christ as the way of salvation."[2] It is one of two ordinances (or practices) of the Protestant Church, with the second being the Lord's Supper.

READ ROMANS 6:1-11. This is a passage we studied in Week One when we considered what it means to be alive in Christ. As you read it again, focus on the baptism elements of Paul's teaching.

What does verse 3 say we are baptized into?

Now look at verse 6. What part of us dies with Christ? What are we freed from by this death?

Compare your life before you believed in Christ with the new life you have in Him. What sinful behaviors and/or patterns of thought do you continue to struggle with and most want to put to death?

Old vs. New

To learn more about the "old self" and its contrast with new life in Christ, pause and read Ephesians 4:20-24 and Colossians 3:1-10.

Sin has a wicked undertow. It pulls us away from abundant life, shackling us to unhealthy ways of living and relating to others. Baptism is a witness to the death of our "old self"—the part of us that resists God's will and gives in to sins like self-centeredness, pride, greed, jealousy, lust, anger, and deceit (just to name a few).

That day when I nearly drowned in the ocean, what I needed more than anything else was someone to grasp my hand and pull me up out of the water. I needed to be rescued. That's precisely what Jesus does—He reaches down and lifts us out of the clutches of sin and death. When we follow Christ in baptism, our journey under the water shows our acceptance of His sacrificial death on our behalf.

> *For if we have been united with him in the likeness of his death, we will certainly also be in the likeness of his resurrection.*

ROMANS 6:5

What a wonderful promise! Romans 6:5 says clearly that if we have died with Christ, then we will surely rise with Him to a life that lasts forever. We are raised "to walk in newness of life" (Romans 6:4). At first, baptism is a snapshot of death, but it quickly becomes a beautiful, enduring portrait of the triumph of resurrection. Death is a fleeting, defeated threat, but life with Christ is eternal.

When a person being baptized is lifted up out of the water, the motion symbolizes that she is being raised up to live with Christ and with the confidence of eternal life in His presence. If you've ever attended a baptism, you probably heard clapping and cheering. There's always a good reason to celebrate a baptism because it symbolizes that a spiritually dead person has been brought back to life forever. For Christians, the grave is not the end. Baptism is a "visible sign of the saving truth of the gospel."[3]

Baptism symbolizes both an ending and a beginning. It is the ending of the old way of life and the beginning of life committed to the mission of God. Jesus Himself began His public ministry by being baptized. Let's take a look together at Jesus's baptism.

TURN TO THE BOOK OF MATTHEW (THE FIRST BOOK OF THE NEW TESTAMENT) AND READ MATTHEW 3:13-17. Why do you think John was hesitant to baptize Jesus (v. 14)?

John's baptism was for repentance from sin, but Jesus was sinless. John knew Jesus was righteous and holy. In fact, he called Jesus "the Lamb of God who would take away the sins of the world" (John 1:29). Jesus didn't need to repent, He didn't need forgiveness, but His mission required Him to be fully obedient to God's will.

 JOHN THE BAPTIST

John was the cousin of Jesus (born to Elizabeth and Zechariah, (Luke 1) who served as the prophet who prepared people for the birth of Jesus the Messiah. John's ministry was focused on repentance (turning from sin) followed by baptism (thus his nickname "the Baptist" or "the Baptizer.") Details about John's life and ministry are found in all four Gospels (Matthew 3; 11; 14; Mark 1; 6; Luke 1; 3; 7; and John 1; 3).

LOOK AGAIN AT MATTHEW 3:15. Why did Jesus encourage John to baptize Him?

Jesus said that His baptism was a way "to fulfill all righteousness." This means "to complete everything that forms part of a relationship of obedience to God."[4] Jesus's baptism was a public statement that He would be wholly obedient to His Father and fulfill every aspect of His mission, including His death and resurrection, which are foreshadowed in the moment of His baptism.

Jesus's baptism marked the start of His public ministry while He was on earth, and He ended His time on earth with a call to baptize those who follow in His footsteps.

READ MATTHEW 28:19-20, WRITTEN BELOW, AND CIRCLE THE PHRASE RELATED TO BAPTISM:

¹⁹Go, therefore, and make disciples of all nations, baptizing them in the name of the Father and of the Son and of the Holy Spirit, ²⁰teaching them to observe everything I have commanded you.

In whose name did Jesus say people should be baptized?

The Great Commission

Matthew 28:18-20 is referred to as the Great Commission because it is Jesus's instruction to His disciples to take over His ministry of making disciples.

We are baptized in the name of the Father, Son, and Spirit—a clear reminder from Jesus that baptism is linked to an understanding of who God is prior to entering into baptism.[5]

Given Jesus's commission before He went back up into heaven, it's no surprise that when we read through the book of Acts (the story of the growth of the early church following Jesus's time on earth), we find a repeated pattern: baptism follows repentance and belief. From the very beginning, when the first churches were being formed, baptism was one of the first steps taken by people who believed in Christ, because it was a public confession of Jesus as Lord.

We've seen that baptism is multifaceted in its meaning. It speaks to faith in Christ and union with Him through death to sin and self. It is a public statement of a commitment to live following the pattern set by Jesus Himself, and so it testifies to an inward transformation of character that has real effects on relationships. It portrays new birth into the body of Christ, identification with the community of faith, and is a step of obedience celebrated by the church. And the motion of rising out of the water anticipates our own resurrection into eternal life (1 Corinthians 15).[6] What a beautiful picture of Jesus's love for you and your commitment to Him.

As you reflect on the meaning of baptism, which of these aspects is most important to you now? Why?

Baptism is a sign that we are alive in Christ! Take a moment to rest in prayer right now and thank the Lord for baptism and all that it symbolizes. If you haven't followed the Lord in baptism yet, ask the Lord if it's time to walk with him through the waters.

Do you have lingering questions about the practice of baptism? If so, write them down here, and find a time to talk about them with your Bible study group leader, a leader in your church, or your pastor.

DAY 03

WE GATHER AT THE TABLE

by Tina Boesch

The bread in my pantry is soft and sliced. If it symbolizes anything, it speaks of the industrialization and efficiency of food production in our time. It's not loaded with meaning like the bread on the table during Jesus's last meal with His disciples—the bread of the Passover.

You'll find an account of Jesus's Last Supper, or at least a mention of the meal's symbolism, in each Gospel book, which is a sure sign for us that it held great significance for Jesus and for the early church. Not only was that meal the last time Jesus ate with His closest friends before the crucifixion, but it took place during one of the most important Jewish festivals of the year—Passover—when Jews remembered and celebrated their exodus from slavery (Exodus 12–13). Reenacting this meal became part of Christian worship as soon as the earliest churches were formed, and it informed the church practice known today as the Lord's Supper.

The Last Supper

Read about the Last Supper in Matthew 26:26-30; Mark 14:22-25; Luke 22:15-20; and John 6:51-58.

LOOK UP AND READ MATTHEW 26:26-30. Next to each item below, write down how Jesus described it to His disciples.

BREAD

CUP

The history and symbolism of Passover may be unfamiliar to us, but every aspect of the meal was meaningful for the disciples. Dishes traditionally served during Passover all recalled aspects of the Israelites' painful experience in Egypt and the wonder of God's rescue. For instance, bitter herbs dipped in salt water were reminiscent of the bitterness of slavery and the tears the people shed before they were freed. The bread on the table would have been made without any yeast to symbolize the desire to eliminate sin and idolatry from hearts, homes, and communities.[7]

When Jesus presented the bread to the disciples, He referred to it as "my body." Do you feel comfortable with the idea of eating someone's flesh? No? None of us can stomach that idea! Our reaction is similar to the way the crowds following Jesus responded when He claimed to be the "bread of life"—some were confused, others offended, and everyone agreed it was a hard teaching (John 6:28-58).

Jesus described how the bread (called manna) God provided to feed the Israelites while they traveled through the wilderness didn't last; it perished. But Jesus said He is, "the living bread that came from heaven." And He continued:

> *[51]If anyone eats of this bread He will live forever. The bread I give for the life of the world is my flesh . . . [54]The one who eats my flesh and drinks my blood has eternal life, and I will raise him up on the last day.*

JOHN 6:51,54

What a stunning promise!

Describe the promise in your own words. What feelings does it evoke in you?

Passover & the Exodus

This part of history is recounted in the Old Testament book of Exodus 5–15, with Exodus 12 describing Passover.

The cup of blood (Matthew 26:27-28), too, is an allusion to the first Passover. The night before the Israelites fled Egypt, they painted the blood of lambs on their door frames so that the angel of death would pass over their homes and spare their first-born sons from death. Lamb's blood may have played a critical role in saving the people from certain death, but it was never something they drank. In fact, the idea of drinking blood was horrific to Jews.

In Jewish law there was a strict prohibition against eating or drinking the blood of animals. Just listen to this law in Leviticus:

> *[13]Any Israelite or alien residing among them, who hunts down a wild animal or bird that may be eaten must drain its blood and cover it with dirt. [14]Since the life of every creature is its blood, I have told the Israelites: You are not to eat the blood of any creature, because the life of every creature is its blood; whoever eats it must be cut off.*

LEVITICUS 17:13-14

What is the prohibition in these verses?

What phrase is repeated?

Jesus's directive to drink His cup, which symbolized His blood, would have been shocking to His disciples (and probably to you too the first time you heard it). But as the author of Leviticus emphasized in verse 14, blood symbolized life. Jesus was speaking symbolically, not literally. Drinking His cup means we're willing to share in His life. The action of drinking the cup during the Lord's Supper is a way of reminding ourselves that Jesus lives in and through us.

During Passover, one of the most important parts of the meal was the lamb. Why do you think Jesus didn't mention it?

In John 1:29, John the Baptist proclaimed, "Look, the Lamb of God, who takes away the sin of the world!" The Passover meal recalled God's deliverance of His people out of the oppression of slavery and His sheltering of them from death. The Lord's Supper reinterprets Passover by acknowledging that Jesus is the ultimate and final Passover lamb whose blood saves us from eternal death. Jesus is our divine Deliverer, His life given freely to give us the hope of eternal life, lived in the presence of God and in the company all those who believe in His Son.[8]

 ## *ORDINANCES OF THE CHURCH*

"Christians agree universally that baptism and the Lord's Supper were instituted by Christ and should be observed as 'ordinances' or 'sacraments' by His followers . . . Christ instituted both ordinances. Both portray publicly and visibly the essential elements of the gospel, and both symbolize realities involving divine activity and human experience. Baptism is a once-for-all experience, but the Lord's Supper is repeated many times. Baptism follows closely one's profession of faith in Christ and actually in the New Testament was the declaration of that faith. The Lord's Supper declares one's continuing dependence upon the Christ proclaimed in the gospel, who died, was buried, and rose for our salvation."[9]

This morning at church, we celebrated the Lord's Supper. My pastor lifted up a flat, round piece of bread and tore it down the middle while repeating Jesus's words in Luke 22:19, "This is my body, which is given for you. Do this in remembrance of me."

When Jesus originally said these words, "He believed that His broken body and His shed blood would bring forgiveness, that His death would turn away God's wrath, and that the whole event, liberating God's people, would usher in the new covenant and the new creation."[10] Jesus wanted us to remember him, to remember all of this—to remember His life, His death, and His resurrection.

Remembrance is a way of recalling a past event to impress its significance for us now. Reenactment is acting out a past event as a way to learn about and celebrate a historical moment.[11] The Lord's Supper is both a remembrance and a reenactment that involves our whole selves. After all, the bread we eat and the cup we drink are tangible, physical elements that literally become part of us. The church is to remember Jesus in this way together—standing, praying, confessing, worshiping. In doing so, we're reminded that we are one body, sisters and brothers who have all found eternal life in Christ.

There is a past, present, and future dimension in this special meal. We remember divine deliverance in the past; we celebrate Jesus's life lived in and through us in the present; and we anticipate the moment when Jesus will return to restore all things once and for all, and we will share this meal with Him.

> **LOOK ONE MORE TIME AT MATTHEW 26:26-30.** When did Jesus say He would drink the fruit of the vine again?

The Lord's Supper is a tiny taste of a delicious banquet awaiting us when Jesus comes again (Revelation 19:6-9).

> Spend some time reflecting on what you've learned today. Which dimension of the Lord's Supper feels most meaningful for you today? If you have lingering questions about the purpose of the Lord's Supper or how it is practiced in your church, note them on the next page and set up a time to talk with someone about them.

Write a short prayer thanking Jesus for the sacrifice this meal symbolizes and His promise of eternal life.

DAY
04

WE
WORSHIP
TOGETHER

by Amy-Jo Girardier

The most effective jingles are the ones that get stuck in your head and you can't ever get them out. My kids have been singing one for a few weeks now that I hear myself humming all the time. I don't want to mention the company because they haven't actually paid for a mention in your Bible study. But the gist of the tune is, "_____, have it your way. You rule!"

I couldn't shake that little jingle as I was writing this session. The idea that we can have it our way—that we sit on the throne of our lives—is a message we all wrestle with. It's a lie that Satan dangles before us just as he did Eve in Genesis 3.

Do you remember the day you realized that wasn't true? The day you knew you weren't King and that you needed to know the One who was?

> Take a moment to reflect on your story of how you came to Jesus. When you have a few minutes today, respond in a journal or on a separate piece of paper: What was your experience with surrendering your life to Jesus and His way?

One of my favorite things about serving at my church is getting to hear people's stories of how they came to know Jesus as King and Savior of their lives. It's happened . . .

> . . . in a parking lot after a church service;
>
> . . . in a backyard during Vacation Bible School;
>
> . . . sitting in the floor of a kitchen on a Sunday afternoon;
>
> . . . in a village in Southeast Asia;
>
> . . . at midnight during a mission trip to Chicago;
>
> . . . in a prison cell;
>
> . . . and on and on.

These times and locations are tied to people who understood that Jesus is King and they are not, so they gave control and ownership of their lives to Him for the rest of their days.

You might be wondering, *What does that have to do with worship?* Everything.

When we gather together to worship God, we remember our salvation stories of how we came to know Him, what He has done for us in saving us, and what He is currently doing in and through our lives. We get to join in with others who have been saved and set free to worship the Living God.

Together we get to say to Him in praise and prayers: "Yes, You are who You say You are. Yes, You do what You say You will do. Yes, You are alive and at work in me and in all of us. Yes, You are Lord and Savior of all our days."

 WORSHIP

Worship is the "expression of reverence and adoration of God." Worship can be private and frequent, like Paul's charge to "present your bodies as a living sacrifice, holy and pleasing to God; this is your true worship." Personal worship happens anytime we pray, delight in the Lord, express gratitude, and so on. Worship can also be corporate, which is what we do when we gather with other believers. Corporate worship is the focus of today's study, but you are privately worshiping God through your Bible study.[12]

FIND PSALM 95 IN YOUR BIBLE AND READ VERSES 1-7A.

Note: When you see "a" or "b" in a Bible verse reference, it's referring to the first half or thought in the verse (a) or the second half or thought in the verse (b).

It's helpful to look at these verses in three parts, in an A-B-A structure.

Part 1 (A) = Psalm 95:1-2

Part 2 (B) = Psalm 95:3-5

Part 3 (A) = Psalm 95:6-7a

The A sections of Psalm 95 describe the acts and attitudes of the worshipers, while B describes the character and work of the One being worshiped.

According to verses 1-2, what are to be the acts and attitudes of the worshipers?

Together with other followers of Christ, we are to joyfully, gratefully, and victoriously lift our voices in praise to the King. And these aren't mere suggestions, these are commands.

What do you observe about God's character and actions that prompts our worship (vv. 3-5)?

Verse 6 instructs the worshiper to "bow down" and "kneel" before God. What does bowing and kneeling symbolize?

Biblical Poetry

These verses from Psalm 95 are an example of the Hebrew poetic feature of synthetic parallelism, "where the idea expressed in the first line of a verse is developed and completed in the following lines."[13]

In 2023, the world had the opportunity to watch the coronation of a new King of England. During that service, Prince William knelt before the new king to pledge his allegiance. Bowing and kneeling indicates humility and submission. It is a recognition that God is the only true King and we have a relationship with Him. We know Him and He is our God. At times, this expression of worship helps us see if we are "kneeling" or "bowing down" before anything else that isn't God. We make idols all the time, but there is only One who truly rules.

If God is our King, that means we are a part of His kingdom—the collective group of those whose allegiance is to Him. We are not in this by ourselves. It's important for us to gather together and worship our King. Why? Good question.

READ HEBREWS 10:24-25,

²⁴And let us consider one another in order to provoke love and good works, ²⁵not neglecting to gather together, as some are in the habit of doing, but encouraging each other, and all the more as you see the day approaching.

Mark the phrases in this passage that mention more than one person together.

The phrase "let us consider" is translated from the Greek word *katanoeō*, which means *to consider attentively, observe, fully, behold, fix one's mind upon*.[14] This word only shows up in the New Testament 14 times. It's hard to consider people, to notice them, when they aren't around. You've heard of the phrase, "Out of sight, out of mind," right?

We live in a world that doesn't worship Jesus as King, which can make personal faithfulness and commitment to Jesus a challenge. That's why we need to be around others who are alive in Christ—to encourage one another, to urge each other on in love and good works.

Here's an experiment: Take your hand and raise it up in the air. Now take your other hand and join it with some force to your raised hand. What happened?

If you're with even one other person and you raise your hand and someone else puts her hand up to yours, that's called a high five. It's a celebration! But you really can't high five yourself. It's just not the same. When it comes to worship, you can (and should) worship God on your own, but you also need others to come alongside of you and they need you to come alongside of them. The corporate, together worship of the body of Christ is a celebratory, challenging, and beautiful picture for the world to see.

Reflect on your current level of worship engagement with others.

Are you showing up regularly at church for worship?

Does your investment level reflect the high priority of corporate worship for the life of a Christ follower?

Where is there room for growth?

This week consider this a new sort of jingle and ask the Lord to get this stuck in your heart and lived out regularly.

"Worship the King who rules, and encourage the others in the kingdom as you do."

Take some time to pray. Sit quietly before the Lord and ask Him to help you see where there is room for growth in your commitment to worshiping regularly with others.

COME, LET'S WORSHIP AND BOW DOWN; LET'S KNEEL BEFORE THE LORD OUR MAKER.

Psalm 95:6

DAY
05

WE SUPPORT THE CHURCH

by Amy-Jo Girardier

When my husband and I were newlyweds, we were moving to Texas for seminary and had no furniture for our apartment. To help us out, my great aunt and uncle from Illinois gave us the weirdest directions. They gave us a box of Illinois tomatoes and told us to go to a particular address in Texas. Once we arrived, we were to give the people who lived there the tomatoes and say we were sent by the Spencers. They promised we would find the furniture we needed if we followed their directions.

My husband and I were skeptical, but when we got to Texas with our box of Illinois tomatoes, we knocked on the door of the address we were given. An elderly couple answered the door and immediately welcomed us into their home. They took our tomatoes and walked us to a large storage building in the backyard. They told us that through the years they had supplied students with furniture to help them set up their homes while they were at seminary. Students would only pay a fraction of the price to rent or purchase the items. They allowed us to just pay in tomatoes.

I will never forget the loving generosity of that couple. They helped so many students like us, called to be leaders in the church, but without any cash to their name.

THE SECOND LETTER TO THE CORINTHIANS

Paul wrote 2 Corinthians to deal with problems within the church and to defend apostolic ministry in general and his apostleship in particular. Second Corinthians is relevant for today in its teachings concerning ministers and their ministries. Among these teachings are the following: 1) God was in Christ reconciling the world to Himself and has given to us a ministry of reconciliation. 2) True ministry in Christ's name involves both suffering and victory. 3) Serving Christ means ministering in His name to the total needs of persons. 4) Leaders in ministry need support and trust from those to whom they minister.[15]

Now look up the New Testament book of 2 Corinthians and **READ 2 CORINTHIANS 9:1-5.**

This is another letter written by the apostle Paul to a church where he had ministered. To whom was Paul bragging about the Corinthians? Why was he commending them?

Why was Paul sending people ahead of him to the Corinthians?

A severe famine in Judea that caused hardship to the Christians in Jerusalem had moved Paul to take up a collection for them. The Corinthian church had made a promise of a generous gift. However, an earlier passage (2 Corinthians 8:10-11) indicates their eagerness to give what they promised was waning. In 2 Corinthians 9, Paul was telling them to finish what they started.

Watch carefully, because Paul was helping them learn the difference between giving their way and giving God's way. Giving our way is like a first-grade word problem. The Corinthians have two offering plates of money, and they give one to the church in Jerusalem. How many offering plates do they have left?

But giving God's way isn't a normal word problem at all.

READ 2 CORINTHIANS 9:10-14.

What math terms do you see in 2 Corinthians 9:10?

What did Paul say would be some of the results from the Corinthians' generous giving?

VERSE 11	
VERSE 12	
VERSE 13	
VERSE 14	

When we give in our own power and from a human perspective, it's a subtraction problem. We focus on what we have or don't have.

When we invite God into the equation and give from His perspective, He multiplies and increases. Paul told the Corinthians that their generous giving would result in the ministry being supported, the gospel being displayed, the giver being moved to thankfulness, and God being glorified.

Our attitude and heart changes about giving when we understand how giving works in God's economy and the kind of givers we're called to be.

LET'S BACKTRACK TO 2 CORINTHIANS 9:6-8.

Where does Paul say the decision to give is made?

And what kind of giver does God love?

Cheerful

The Greek word translated cheerful is hilaros and it also means "joyous, prompt to do anything."[16]

I love this truth! It doesn't say God loves a big giver but a cheerful one. God knows that the decision to give cheerfully is not really about the condition of our finances but the condition of our hearts. And what should move our hearts to give is to realize how freely God has given to us. In the previous chapter, Paul gave us the best model to follow:

> *For you know the grace of our Lord Jesus Christ: though he was rich, for your sake he became poor, so that by his poverty you might become rich.*

2 CORINTHIANS 8:9

Take a moment to lay your time, money, abilities, and other resources before the Lord. Ask Him how He wants you to give. Maybe He's calling you:

- To give your time to serve with children or students in your church?

- To give regularly to support the ministry of your church?

- To open your home to someone in need of a temporary place to live?

- Or something else.

What is God saying to you about your giving?

Hold your time, talents, and treasures in open hands to Him and cheerfully ask Him to use them to grow the kingdom of God.

READ EPHESIANS 3:20-21.

20Now to him who is able to do above and beyond all that we ask or think according to the power that works in us— 21to him be glory in the church and in Christ Jesus to all generations, forever and ever. Amen.

I use this beautiful prayer of Paul's with people I serve with at church as we go on mission journeys or serve in various ways. It's a prayer putting everything in God's hands and knowing He will get the glory as He does more than we could ever imagine.

As you close the day, open both of your hands and pray Ephesians 3:20-21, or something in your own words, like the following:

"Jesus, I want to be a cheerful giver. Help me see you work in and through my gifts of time, talents, and treasures for your glory."

Doxology

Ephesians 3:20-21 is an example of a doxology, "A brief formula for expressing praise or glory to God."[17]

REFLECT

Take a few minutes to reflect on the truths you uncovered in your study of God's Word this week. Journal any final thoughts below, or use the space to take notes during your Bible study group conversation. The three questions on the opposite page can be used for your personal reflection or group discussion.

_____

_____

_____

_____

_____

_____

_____

_____

_____

_____

_____

_____

_____

_____

_____

_____

_____

_____

_____

_____

_____

_____

Leading a group? Download the *Alive* leader guide at **lifeway.com/alive**.

As you reflect on the Bible passages you read this week, what stands out to you about the character of God?

How have you been challenged and encouraged in your relationship with Jesus through what you've learned?

Write down one way you can use what you've learned this week to encourage someone else.

Journey
LIVING AS
A CHRISTIAN

Set your minds on things above,
not on earthly things.

COLOSSIANS 3:2

Daily life as a follower of Christ looks different than life apart from Him, but how? In this week of study, we'll consider some of the most important aspects of walking with Jesus, such as prayer, Bible study, loving people well, and sharing about Jesus with others. Jesus invites you into a lifelong journey of faith and friendship.

DAY 01

TALKING
WITH
GOD

by Eunice J. Chung Carlson

What comes to mind when you think about prayer? Your answer is probably somewhere between overwhelmed and overjoyed. Prayer is an amazing and precious gift, yet sometimes it can feel strange, like you're talking into thin air. Or it could feel pointless, saying things to God who already knows everything. Thankfully, we have invaluable teachings from Jesus that help us better understand what it means to pray, along with why and how we need to be constantly conversing with our heavenly Father.

THE GOSPEL OF LUKE

The Gospel of Luke is the third book in the New Testament. Like all four Gospels, the book is about Jesus's earthly ministry and His role as the Messiah. Luke also wrote the book of Acts, which picks up where Luke's Gospel leaves off and focuses on the spread of the church after Jesus returned to heaven.

FIND THE GOSPEL OF LUKE IN YOUR BIBLE AND THEN READ LUKE 11:1-13. How would you describe what prayer is from this passage?

Is it not so kind of the Lord to want us to talk to Him? Just as a loving and attentive dad delights in his kids talking to him, God, our heavenly Father, wants to hear our prayers. Jesus urges us to be bold and persistent in our prayers. We are to continue to ask, seek, and knock—to constantly be in conversation with God. He is listening and will respond to us.

This doesn't mean God gives us everything we want. No good parent does. But what is evident in this passage is that God desires to give good gifts to His children. If an earthly father wants to bless his children, how much more does the heavenly Father want to do so? The Father's graciousness in giving is beautifully displayed by giving us Himself in the presence of the Holy Spirit.

What request of God has been in your prayers for a long time? Do you find encouragement in this passage to keep praying? Explain your thoughts.

Prayer

"Prayer in the Bible involves the dialogue between God and people . . . Prayer will lead to a greater communion with God and a greater understanding of His will."[1]

God has ordained it that He works through the prayers of His people. He is all-powerful and all-knowing, yet this majestic God has determined that He involves us in the accomplishment of His will. Our prayers matter! Prayer is talking with God, and it has supernatural ramifications.

Now flip back two books to the Gospel of Matthew and **READ MATTHEW 6:5-8.**

In this passage, Jesus warned about praying like two different groups of people. Use the chart below to list the group, the warning, and the solution/reason.

VERSES	GROUP	PRAYER PROBLEM	SOLUTION/ REASON
5-6			
7-8			

Prayer shouldn't be something used to draw attention to yourself or to show off. Neither should you think that the more words you use puts you in better standing with God. Instead, Jesus said we should pray humbly and understand that God knows what we need.

Reread the statements from Jesus's teaching printed below. Mark the three-word phrase they have in common.

He said to them, "Whenever you pray, say, Father, your name be honored as holy. Your kingdom come."

LUKE 11:2

Whenever you pray, you must not be like the hypocrites, because they love to pray standing in the synagogues and on the street corners to be seen by people. Truly I tell you, they have their reward.

MATTHEW 6:5

Based on what you just marked, what is Jesus's expectation for His followers regarding prayer?

Jesus started the conversation about prayer in both passages with "whenever you pray" (also translated "when you pray"). Jesus expected prayer to be a regular habit of His followers—not an option but a regular habit.

Jesus not only talked about prayer, He showed His disciples how to pray with a model prayer. You may hear this example referred to as "the Lord's Prayer." Christians have used and recited it for centuries. It's a beautiful prayer not meant just to memorize and repeat, but to be an example on how to pray.

READ THE LORD'S PRAYER IN MATTHEW 6:9-13.
Note one or two takeaways you have about prayer from reading Jesus's example.

Holy

To say God is holy means He is set apart or unique from all of creation (Exodus 15:11). It also speaks to "his absolute purity or goodness. This means that he is untouched and unstained by the evil in the world."[2]

The prayer begins in Matthew 6:9 with a recognition that God is our holy Father and is in heaven. The use of "our" here is a helpful reminder for us that this is a prayer for all Christians everywhere. God is to be revered and worshiped for He is holy. We should begin our prayers with a time of worship before our Father where we recognize who He is.

Matthew 6:10 asks for God's kingdom and will to be done here on earth just as it is in heaven. Jesus instructs us to ask God to accomplish His will in our world. The Lord's Prayer continues in 6:11 with a request for God to provide our daily bread, our daily needs. The Lord's Prayer gives us space to recognize and verbalize our needed dependence on God. We must acknowledge that He, not ourselves, is the Provider.

The next lines of the Lord's Prayer challenge us to forgive. Just as we have experienced life-altering forgiveness from God through Christ, we are to have this attitude toward others. The Lord's Prayer concludes asking for God's protection to keep us away from temptation and evil. We need God's grace to resist the devil and be shielded from the evil one, and God promises to help us when we ask.

> Which lines of the Lord's Prayer stick out to you in your current situation or circumstance? Why?

The Lord's Prayer is not an incantation or filled with magic words. It's not something we can utter by rote and routine to get what we want. However, it is a model to help us pray. In teaching us this prayer, Jesus wasn't just telling us what to pray, but how to pray.[3] In times when we may not know what to pray, or when we grow weary in prayer, the Lord's Prayer can serve as a rubric for us and a gentle reminder of who we're praying to: His holiness, His kingship, His provision, His forgiveness, and His protection. It is a gift. Thank you, Lord!

> What have you learned about prayer today that will help you have a more effective prayer life?

Close with prayer, using the Lord's Prayer as a model.

OUR FATHER IN
HEAVEN, YOUR
NAME BE HONORED
AS HOLY. YOUR
KINGDOM COME.
YOUR WILL BE
DONE ON EARTH AS
IT IS IN HEAVEN.

Matthew 6:9-10

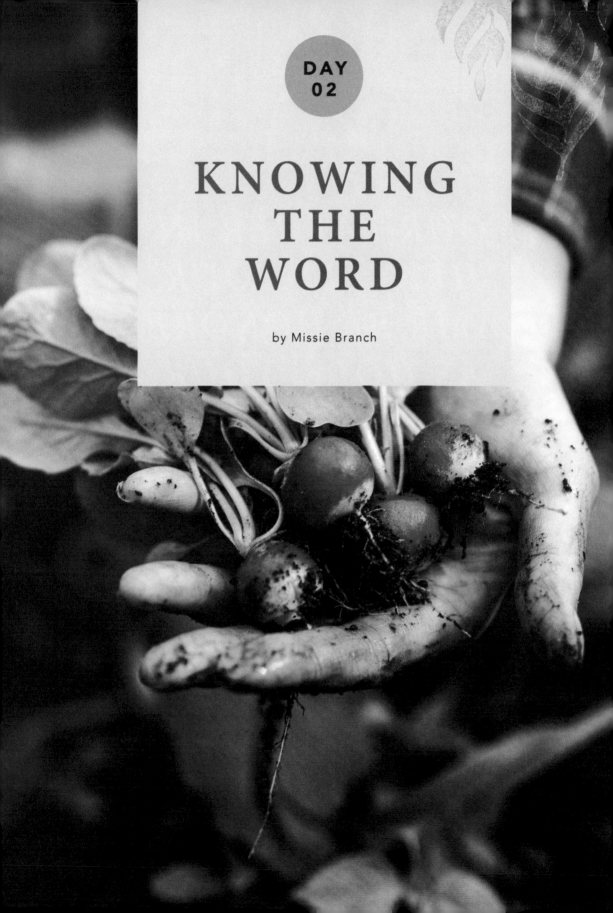

KNOWING
THE
WORD

by Missie Branch

In the morning before I get ready for work, I get up, put on my robe and slippers, pour a cup of coffee, sit in my favorite chair, and I talk to the Lord. I have tried many different morning routines, but this is the one that I enjoy the most. The opportunity to talk with the God who I've walked with for more than thirty years is still as awe inspiring to me today as it was when I first believed.

As I talk to the Lord, I try to spend part of this time reciting back to Him what He has said to us in His Word. The Bible is called God's Word because it literally contains the words of God for the people of God. In it we are given access to the Father's plan for a lost humanity, the Son's mission to rescue and restore us, and the Spirit's protection over us.

 THE HOLY BIBLE

The Bible is God's Word, written by the men God inspired to write it. Through it, God reveals Himself to us. "It is a perfect treasure of divine instruction. It has God for its author, salvation for its end, and truth, without any mixture of error, for its matter. Therefore, all Scripture is totally true and trustworthy. It reveals the principles by which God judges us, and therefore is, and will remain to the end of the world, the true center of Christian union, and the supreme standard by which all human conduct, creeds, and religious opinions should be tried. All Scripture is a testimony to Christ, who is Himself the focus of divine revelation."[4]

Very close to the middle of the Bible you'll find a psalm that's whole purpose is to celebrate the beautiful gift that is the Word of God—Psalm 119. At that point in history, the psalmist would have had only the earliest books of the Bible in view, which were known as the Torah (Genesis, Exodus, Leviticus, Numbers, and Deuteronomy). But as readers today, we can delight in God's full written Word.

PSALM 119:41-48

⁴¹Let your faithful love come to me, Lord,
your salvation, as you promised.

⁴²Then I can answer the one who taunts
me,
for I trust in your word.

⁴³Never take the word of truth from my
mouth,
for I hope in your judgments.

⁴⁴I will always obey your instruction,
forever and ever.

⁴⁵I will walk freely in an open place
because I study your precepts.

⁴⁶I will speak of your decrees before kings
and not be ashamed.

⁴⁷I delight in your commands,
which I love.

⁴⁸I will lift up my hands to your
commands,
which I love,
and will meditate on your statutes.

PSALM 119:97-105

⁹⁷How I love your instruction!
It is my meditation all day long.

⁹⁸Your command makes me wiser than my
enemies,
for it is always with me.

⁹⁹I have more insight than all my teachers
because your decrees are my meditation.

¹⁰⁰I understand more than the elders
because I obey your precepts.

¹⁰¹I have kept my feet from every evil path
to follow your word.

¹⁰²I have not turned from your judgments,
for you yourself have instructed me.

¹⁰³How sweet your word is to my taste—
sweeter than honey in my mouth.

¹⁰⁴I gain understanding from your
precepts;
therefore I hate every false way.

¹⁰⁵Your word is a lamp for my feet
and a light on my path.

READ PSALM 119:41-48 AND PSALM 119:97-105, PRINTED ON THE OPPOSITE PAGE. AS YOU READ THESE VERSES:

Underline every "I" statement the writer makes.

Circle each description of God's Word.

I've done the first one to get you started.

In Psalm 119, we're given a glimpse into the heart of a regular person whose spiritual life has been transformed by spending time learning from God in His Word. These verses teach that each of us are given access to salvation, good judgment, discernment, wisdom beyond our years, instruction, understanding, insight, and God's faithful love. Spending time in God's Word prevents following evil and has answers for being offended.

What do you think it means for the Word of God to be a light for your path (v. 105)? Rewrite this verse in your own words.

How have you seen this proven true?

As a light or a lamp, we can look to God's Word for daily guidance and direction on how to live in a manner that glorifies God and accomplishes His will for us. What a generous gift. But to enjoy this gift fully, there is a cost. The price is time and commitment. The author of this psalm makes it clear that all this gain, all this connection, is the byproduct of an investment in God's Word. The author is meditating on it, studying it, delighting in it, obeying it, and loving it. There is an active pursuit of God's Word resulting in a vibrant spiritual life. And when we are transformed spiritually, our daily lives will be impacted. Attitudes, actions, work, relationships, and emotions are made new.

Hearing God's Word is the simplest way to take it all in. This can be done through both listening to sermons and reading it out loud. In addition to hearing it, Christians need to spend time reading and learning the Bible. Taking the first steps can be confusing at first. Where do you start? What do you need to know? One easy way is to start at the beginning. The Bible is one big story about God, beginning in the book of Genesis and ending in the book of Revelation. God is inviting you into His story, and He will meet you there in the pages of this book.

Once you've started your lifelong journey through God's Word, there are a few things I want you to consider:

MAKE TIME. As believers in Christ, we must be devoted to regularly reading God's Word (Matthew 4:4). As we read, we better understand what it means to be women who love God, live for Him, and then show His love to others. I mentioned at the start of today that the mornings have become my time, but it may look different for you. It could be evenings, lunch breaks, carpool lines, audio at the gym or on a commute, or some combination. There is no "winning" formula; what matters is that you make time to be in God's Word every day.

NEXT, COMMIT TO MEMORIZING AND MEDITATING. Memorizing Scripture strengthens your faith (Psalm 119:11). As you store God's Word in your mind, it becomes accessible to you throughout your day-to-day life.

STUDY THE TEXT. This is digging in, unearthing, and finding the biblical gems. Regular reading of God's Word expands us like the beautiful canopy of a tree. But committed studying of God's Word makes us deeper like the roots that go down into the soil to feed and support the canopy (2 Timothy 3:14-17). The more we understand God's Word, the more we understand His heart, His purposes, and who He desires for us to be.

TEST IT. This is where you apply what you've learned. Being in God's Word requires a response (James 1:22). After you've spent time in the Bible, you should be able to recognize at least one clear response that you'll make to what you've read. Commit yourself to at least one action to take regardless of how big or small it may seem.

DON'T GO IT ALONE. One of the great beauties of the Christian faith is that God desires for us to grow in Him together. He is relational at heart, as seen through the Trinity relationships between Father, Son, and Spirit. It's not up to you to mine the truths of Scripture on your own—take advantage of the wisdom of those who have gone before you and the community available to you today (Ephesians 2:19-21).

Every day is filled with pressure, temptation, and decisions. The Bible provides the wisdom to face them all. God's character is trustworthy, and His promises are true. We reflect this in our lives as we allow Him to be the influencer effecting our thinking and behavior. A commitment to studying the Bible is one of the most impactful investments you can make in your relationship with Jesus and your spiritual growth.

What is one way you want to commit to being in God's Word daily? Write it here.

Now think of someone who can help you follow through on this commitment, someone who can join you and encourage you in your study. Reach out to that person today and come up with a plan together. You'll be so glad you did!

Read all of Psalm 119 as a prayer of gratitude and worship to God for the gift of His Word.

DAY
03

BATTLING SIN

by Michelle Hicks

When I taught in the Kids Ministry at my church, explaining sin was always a fun topic with kids. We tried to keep the concepts concrete and clear. One illustration we used was some kind of fun game involving a target. That gave us the opportunity to talk about Romans 3:23, where it says, "All have sinned and fall short of the glory of God." The word for *sin* means to "miss the mark."[5] Unfortunately, we all miss the mark more often than we care to admit.

Now, let's review a few important truths from our first two weeks of study: As believers in Christ, all our sins—past, present, and future—are forgiven. Through the cross, God exchanged our sinfulness for the righteousness of Christ (Week 1, Day 3). Because of that we are justified forever (Week 1, Day 4). Our relationship with Him is secure and our sin is no longer counted against us (Week 2, Day 4).

All of these things are true. However, we still live in a world broken by sin, and our earthly bodies are still prone to sin. We're still tempted and we still fall sometimes. Since all of those things remain true, how can we live in obedience to God? How can we not let sin get the best of us?

STAND ON THE WORD

First, let's consider how Jesus dealt with temptation.

READ MATTHEW 4:1-11.

Where was Jesus and what did He face while He was there?

How did the devil tempt Jesus and how did Jesus respond each time?

TEMPTATION	RESPONSE

You might ask: "Why did the Holy Spirit lead Jesus into the wilderness to be tempted by the devil in the first place?" While Jesus is fully divine, He is also fully human. To be the Savior and Lord we need Him to be, He had to experience all things human. Temptation is one of those experiences. He faced it, but didn't sin. How? What did He use to combat the temptation? The Word of God.

We can do the same.

In **PSALM 119:9-11,** we read,

> *⁹How can a young man keep his way pure?*
> *By keeping your word.*
>
> *¹⁰I have sought you with all my heart;*
> *don't let me wander from your commands.*
>
> *¹¹I have treasured your word in my heart*
> *so that I may not sin against you.*

How did the psalmist say we win the battle against sin?

What does it mean to treasure God's word in your heart?

When we internalize Scripture through practices like study, meditation, and memorization, we come to know—to truly understand—the teachings of God's Word. We can reflect on or repeat Scripture in the face of temptation. This gives us truth to stand on in the face of the enemy's lies.

And one Scripture we should hold close in this temptation battle is **1 CORINTHIANS 10:13,**

> *No temptation has come upon you except what is common to humanity.*
> *But God is faithful, he will not allow you to be tempted beyond what you are*
> *able, but with the temptation he will also provide the way out so that you may be*
> *able to bear it.*

This verse is a great reminder we are not in this alone. God has not saved us just to throw us out into the world to fend for ourselves until we go to heaven. He is with us. Watching over us. Providing for us. Empowering us to be victorious.

LIVE DIFFERENTLY

God's Word also reminds us that we are no longer slaves to sin but slaves to God when we trust Jesus as Savior and Lord (see Romans 6:15-22). Through the power of the Holy Spirit in us we are empowered to let go of the old life of sin and instead live a new life in Christ.

> **TURN TO THE BOOK OF EPHESIANS AND READ EPHESIANS 4:17-24.** How is the old way of life described in these verses?

> What are we to do to walk in this new way of life (vv. 20-24)?

Though we have been changed through the power of Christ, it's hard to give up old habits. If we're not careful, we'll find ourselves living in a way that reflects our old way of life, rather than the new. But Paul called us to be intentional in walking the new life.

- Take off your former way of life (v. 22).

- Be renewed in the spirit of your minds (v. 23).

- Put on the new self (v. 24).

We are not passive participants in walking out this new life. As we grow in Christ, study and learn Scripture, and yield to the Spirit's leadership in our lives, we must choose to live differently.

NOW READ EPHESIANS 4:25-32. As you read, list some of the different behaviors we are to choose as we follow Christ.

Look more closely at verse 25. What role do other Christians play in our battle against sin (v. 25)?

The change God makes in our lives will be evident. We can look at the fruit of our lives—our words, actions, attitudes, motives, behaviors, feelings, thoughts—and recognize if we are living according to the old life or the new. We will know it and others will notice it too. Through the power of the Spirit, we are slowly but steadily being transformed to look more like Jesus.

The battle with sin is one we will deal with until we see Christ. But we are not in it alone. One of the blessings of Christian community is the ability to confess our sins to others and to speak truth into one another's lives. In the dark of our personal battles, our sins often fester. But when brought out into the light through confession and vulnerability, they lose their power.

Take a few minutes to consider the following:

What have you learned today that will help you with the constant battle with temptation and sin?

What is the next step you need to take to walk in the new way of life you have in Christ?

Practice confession and repentance now as you pray. Then praise God for the truth that being alive in Christ means you can experience victory over sin both today and eventually forever.

I HAVE TREASURED YOUR WORD IN MY HEART SO THAT I MAY NOT SIN AGAINST YOU.

Psalm 119:11

DAY
04

LOVING
PEOPLE

by Erin Franklin

When I was two years old, my mom and I were watching a home video of my family which had been filmed several years prior to grandchildren arriving, so the video featured only adults. I am the second oldest of all the cousins. (My cousin A.J. is about six months older than I am.) Since A.J. is older, he has always been in my life, just as every other person in the video had always been in my life. So, I was very confused as to why A.J. was not in the video.

"Where's Yay Yay?" I asked my mom. (Yay Yay was my two-year-old self's name for A.J.)

"A.J. wasn't born yet," my mom explained. She then tried to untangle to my two-year-old mind how he wasn't born and then was born. "Do you understand?" she asked.

"Yes," I nodded my head confidently.

A few moments passed, then I asked again, "Where's Yay Yay?"

Similarly, understanding the intricacies of the Christian faith can feel unfamiliar and at times confusing, especially if you didn't grow up in a church environment. Trying to learn new terminology and unfamiliar doctrines (the central beliefs of Christianity) can feel overwhelming. Just when you think you've got it all down, a new concept pops up and you're asking the same questions again.

Love is the foundation of the Christian faith, but sometimes, a concept even as foundational as love can feel challenging. We are commanded to love each other as Jesus loved us (John 15:12), but what does that mean? Am I really supposed to lay down my life for the people in my church? And Jesus said I'm also to love my enemies and pray for them. Seriously? We'll consider these questions and more as we see what the Bible tells us about loving others.

LOVING THOSE LIKE ME

Twice in John's Gospel, Jesus told His followers that they were to love each other as He had loved them (John 13:34; 15:12). But what does that look like?

God Is Love

Love is at the heart of Christian relationships because it is at the core of God's own nature (1 John 4:8).

READ THE FOLLOWING EXCERPT FROM THE BOOK OF 1 JOHN.

¹⁶This is how we have come to know love: He laid down his life for us. We should also lay down our lives for our brothers and sisters. ¹⁷If anyone has this world's goods and sees a fellow believer in need but withholds compassion from him—how does God's love reside in him? ¹⁸Little children, let us not love in word or speech, but in action and in truth.

1 JOHN 3:16-18

What did John say defines love?

How are we to reflect that kind of sacrificial love?

Our love for brothers and sisters in Christ is to be a sacrificial love modeled after the life-giving, sacrificial love of Jesus for us. We are to give to one another, to meet each other's needs, and yes, sacrifice even to the point of giving our physical lives for each other. Our love is to be extreme and extravagant. It's a love that is not just heard but seen.

Now turn in your Bible to the New Testament book of Colossians (one of Paul's letters). **READ COLOSSIANS 3:12-17.**

Paul listed several character traits that are to be part of the Christian life. According to verse 14, what did Paul say is the most important characteristic to put on? Why is that so?

In verse 14, Paul noted that love is to be the chief character trait of the Christian life because it "is the perfect bond of unity." So, in the church, there is no better way to come together—to be unified—than by loving each other. As brothers and sisters in Christ, we are a family of believers, so our behavior should exemplify a loving family—one that shows kindness, patience, and compassion toward each other. A family that builds each other up, bears with one another, and forgives each other. Though members of the family may not always be in complete agreement on everything, their foundation of love makes them strong.

Is this the kind of love displayed in your church? Explain. What can you do to foster this kind of love?

List a few ideas of ways you could love others by serving in your local church.

During His time on earth, Jesus set forth an example of humbling Himself and meeting the needs of others. Demonstrating love in the church often looks the same—humbling ourselves and serving others.

LOVING THOSE WHO DON'T LIKE ME

We understand the call to love our brothers and sisters in Christ, those who are like us, and most of the time like us. But what about people who don't like us? Are we supposed to love them too?

LOOK UP AND READ MATTHEW 5:43-48.

How did Jesus say we are to treat our enemies?

What did Jesus give as the reason we are to obey this command?

How is it possible for us to do this?

The Sermon on the Mount

These verses from Matthew 5 are part of Jesus's "Sermon on the Mount" (Matthew 5–7), a teaching about what it looks like to live as a citizen of God's kingdom.

No Excuse

The Bible is clear that loving one's enemy isn't the same as staying in manipulative, abusive, or any way harmful situations. There is no room for the mistreatment of others in the kingdom of God (Isaiah 1:17; Proverbs 22:8).

It's not out of the ordinary to love those who are kind to us, who are generous and forgiving. But as Christians, we are called to a higher standard—to humble ourselves and love even our enemies. In doing so, we are reflecting the love God has shown to each of us. And we are reflecting His character. But it is impossible for us to do this in our own power.

When God calls us, He also equips us. To love others like Jesus does, we can only do so through the Holy Spirit who empowers us. As we grow as Christians, He changes us to be more like Jesus. To see others as Christ sees them. To love them despite how they speak of us or treat us. This may not be easy at times, but it is what we are called to do.

> Is there anyone you're currently struggling to love? A difficult person? An enemy? What is a step toward love you need to take today, either in your heart or in action?

If you live in this tension of finding it hard to love someone yet wanting to obey Jesus, a great first step is to pray. Be honest with the Lord about your feelings and your desire to live by His Word. Ask Him to love that person through you. And begin to pray for the person you're struggling with. There's something about praying for someone that melts your heart toward them.

Practicing an attitude of love is not always easy, sometimes even toward those like you and who like you. But we are to love as Jesus loved us. It's not a request, it's a command. Thankfully, with the Holy Spirit living in us, it is possible.

Use your closing time in prayer to pray for specific relationships that have come to mind throughout your time in God's Word today.

*LITTLE CHILDREN,
LET US NOT
LOVE IN WORD
OR SPEECH,
BUT IN ACTION
AND IN TRUTH.*

1 John 3:18

DAY
05

LIVING
ON
MISSION

by Y Bonesteele

In one of Jesus's most famous teachings, the Sermon on the Mount, Jesus used two different word pictures to illustrate the Christian life— "the salt of the earth" and "the light of the world" (Matthew 5:13-16). Both of these pictures speak to how the life of a Christ follower is supposed to look distinctly different from the life of a person who doesn't know Jesus. The goal, in Jesus's words, is for His followers to "let your light shine before others, so that they may see your good works and give glory to your Father in heaven" (Matthew 5:16).

Living a life that glorifies God is about modeling the joy and hope you've found in Jesus so that others will want to know and be like Jesus, too. You may hear this referred to as "living on mission" for Jesus or "making disciples." It's about obedience to Jesus's Great Commission, the charge to go and make disciples (Matthew 28:19-20; Week 3, Day 2). This takes intentionality, sacrifice, and creativity in our already busy lives. The apostle Paul, whose New Testament writings are some of the most helpful instructions on the Christian life, refers to it as being an ambassador for Jesus.

> Look up the term *ambassador* in an online dictionary and write the definition here.

Glorifying God

"'Glorifying' means feeling and thinking and acting in ways that reflect [God's] greatness, that make much of God, that give evidence of the supreme greatness of all his attributes and the all-satisfying beauty of his manifold perfections."[6]

LOOK UP AND READ 2 CORINTHIANS 5:17-21. Paul uses descriptive language here to describe the basis of the Christian faith. In your own words, what has God done for you through Christ (verses 17-19)?

When we become Christ followers, we are transformed from "death" (separation from God) to "life" (relationship with God). When Jesus died on the cross and rose again, He made it possible for people to go from being God's enemies to being members of His family. This is what Paul was referring to when he described our being reconciled to Christ.

Because of our own relationship with Jesus, we see the world differently and we have a mission to live like Jesus, counter culturally. We no longer live for ourselves, but for Him, as His ambassadors—people who represent Him to the world. We understand that "everything is from God" (v. 18)— our finances, our friendships, our family, our jobs, our time, and our gifts our time, and our gifts and talents. And we've been given a new purpose: the ministry of reconciliation—using everything God has given us to help others be drawn back to Him as well.

One way to carry this message of reconciliation is to share your personal testimony, your coming-to-Christ story. Every personal testimony has three parts: 1) What my old life was like before Jesus; 2) how I met Jesus; and 3) what my new life is like now.

> Take five minutes now to reflect on your personal story of how you came to know Jesus.
>
> Think of one person you can share your story with and write that person's name here: _____. Begin praying for an opportunity to talk with that person and for the confidence to speak up when the opportunity comes.

No matter the details—if you came to Christ as a child, or a month ago—yours is a beautiful testimony of the love and hope found in Jesus. You can use your story to help others understand that trouble, sadness, and sin may still come in and out of our lives, but God is faithful to His promise to be with us. As we tell our stories, the message of the cross takes center stage, and God will do the changing of hearts in His time.

In college, I led a small Bible study that wanted to provide free snacks for our dorm during finals week. At first, there was only a trickle of students coming for the snacks. Nobody believed it was true—that poor college students would provide anything free, let alone coveted snacks during finals week. We had a simple message: "We just want to serve people like Jesus serves us." The news spread, people were appreciative, and we ended up adding two new people to our Bible study.

When we live on mission, we take time to think about the people we daily encounter—neighbors, or people we see at the gym, a mom's club, a coffee shop we frequent, or a booster club. Decide on something you enjoy and would naturally want to do anyway and invite others to join you. As they walk in relationship with you, and see your life following Jesus, they will find something attractive about Jesus and your life in Him. Living on mission, then, is about seeing the world through Jesus's eyes, meeting needs—physical, emotional, mental, and spiritual—to see the kingdom of God grow.

BEFORE YOU WRAP UP, READ JOHN 20:21.

Jesus said to them again, "Peace be with you. As the Father has sent me, I also send you."

When Jesus greeted the disciples after His resurrection, He said, "Peace be with you," as a greeting and an encouragement to remind them not to be anxious, knowing God was with them. And when Jesus said, "As the Father sent me, I also send you," He was showing a pattern of how we are to follow in His steps.

In the original language of the Bible, the "you" is a plural, a "you all." Jesus is sending us all—every Christian—and we are to fulfill His mission to reach the world alongside others just as He did. He gives the Holy Spirit to guide and strengthen us as well. Through these verses, He shows that we are following a pattern of following Christ as He follows the Father, doing so with the help of those around us and the help of the Holy Spirit. Living for Jesus is best done together, as the body of believers support each other on mission, making it easier than we think it can be.

> What big or small endeavor can you put on your calendar this week to live as an ambassador of Christ? Who can you partner with?

Living on mission is not a task, it's a lifestyle. For God knows that when we partner with Him to reconcile people to Himself, our joy and purpose will feel full. God doesn't need us. Being all-powerful, He could do it all Himself. But He gives us the privilege of working alongside Him, that we may feel the blessings of seeing others come to Jesus. And what a great privilege and thrill for us, for "how beautiful are the feet of those who bring good news" (Romans 10:15).

Take a moment to pray: Lord, when I try to share about You, I don't always know what to say or do and am afraid I might mess up. Give me boldness to speak Your name and to love radically, that others may come to know the same joy in knowing You.

REFLECT

Take a few minutes to reflect on the truths you uncovered in your study of God's Word this week. Journal any final thoughts below, or use the space to take notes during your Bible study group conversation. The three questions on the opposite page can be used for your personal reflection or group discussion.

_____

_____

_____

_____

_____

_____

_____

_____

_____

_____

_____

_____

_____

_____

_____

_____

_____

_____

_____

_____

_____

_____

_____

Leading a group? Download the *Alive* leader guide at **lifeway.com/alive**.

As you reflect on the Bible passages you read this week, what stands out to you about the character of God?

How have you been challenged and encouraged in your relationship with Jesus through what you've learned?

Write down one way you can use what you've learned this week to encourage someone else.

Forever

OUR FUTURE HOPE

Let us run with endurance the race that lies before us, keeping our eyes on Jesus, the pioneer and perfecter of our faith.

HEBREWS 12:1-2

Life with Christ changes who we are and how we live today, but it also has a profound impact on our future. Through Jesus we gain the promise of eternal life with God—life forever in His presence and away from the sin and sorrow of our world. This is the future hope we cling to, and it impacts everything from how we face suffering and death to our motivation for sharing Jesus with others and leaving behind a legacy of faithfulness. We are to live with the end in mind, and what a beautiful end it is.

DAY
01

ENDURE
TO
THE END

by Nikki Lawrence

Just by pure definition, the word *endurance* likely does not make any of our hearts leap with excitement. *Webster's Dictionary* defines *endurance* as "the ability to withstand hardship or adversity."[1] It ultimately means we've had to press through something difficult and battle our way to a finish line. Who wants to sign up for that? But as we'll see in today's study, we are actually equipped by God to endure, there is spiritual growth that awaits us as we persevere within our Christian race, and most importantly, in Jesus, we have the perfect example of One who has endured and shows us the way forward.

THE LETTER TO THE HEBREWS & THE FAITHFUL BEFORE US

The epistle to the Hebrews is a tribute to the incomparable Son of God and an encouragement to the author's persecuted fellow believers. The author feared that his Christian readers were wavering in their endurance. The writer had a twofold approach. 1) He exalted Jesus Christ, who is addressed as both "God" and "the Son of Man," and is thus the only one who can serve as mediator between God and humanity. 2) He exhorted his fellow Christians to "go on to maturity" and live "by faith."[2]

THEY THAT ENDURED

At the beginning of Hebrews 12, the unknown author of this New Testament book penned these words,

> [1]*Therefore, since we also have such a large cloud of witnesses surrounding us, let us lay aside every hindrance and the sin that so easily ensnares us. Let us run with endurance the race that lies before us,* [2]*keeping our eyes on Jesus, the pioneer and perfecter of our faith. For the joy that lay before him, he endured the cross, despising the shame, and sat down at the right hand of the throne of God.*

HEBREWS 12:1-2

Hebrews 12 opens with a picture of a large crowd of witnesses surrounding us and encouraging us to run with endurance the race—the Christian life of faithful obedience—set before us. The crowd the author is referring to can be found one chapter earlier in Hebrews 11, in a passage often referred to as the "hall of faith" for its list of individuals whose lives model faithfulness to God for us. (If you have time now, find Hebrews 11 in your Bible and read it as well.) These individuals walked through a range of significant trials during their lives but persevered in obedience to the Lord, to the point that He holds them up as models for us.

> The writer of Hebrews describes the Christian life as a race, a visual image Paul also uses (1 Corinthians 9). In what ways is life like a race?

> When you think about a life of faithfulness to God in particular, what does the race imagery mean to you?

Whether reading about Noah, who built an ark in faith despite the ridicule of those around him, or Sarah, who was well past child-bearing years and struggled to believe she would ever give birth, these believers experienced hardship, and God was faithful. Despite challenges, each of them proceeded in faith believing that God would do what He promised. These heroes of the faith are a testament even now of God's faithfulness in difficulty.

With the race imagery, the writer emphasizes the long view of the Christian life, a life lived in seeming opposition to the values and culture of the world around us. Depending on where we live and the people we're surrounded with, we will face varying degrees of persecution for our faith. Jesus told us to expect this as His followers (John 16:33). However, like the Old Testament witnesses show us, we can trust God's faithfulness to us just the same.

> **READ BACK OVER HEBREWS 12:2.** List everything this one verse tells you about the example of faithful endurance Jesus set. What stands out to you?

In Hebrews 12:2, we are pointed to Jesus. His example of the ultimate endurance gives us a role model to follow. We are reminded of our Savior's own perseverance as He experienced the fullness of betrayal, rejection, and persecution—yet endured the cross. We remember that no matter what we are going through, there is no greater suffering than what Jesus experienced in our place and for our sake.

Christ's example strengthens us for our own journeys of faith and reminds us that He empathizes with our call to persevere.

HOW WE ENDURE

NOW LOOK UP AND READ 2 PETER 1:3-8.

As we contemplate the testimonies of the witnesses we read about earlier and consider the charge to lay aside the sin that so easily entraps us, we quickly realize that none of it is possible in our own strength. The days can be hard and temptation to stray can feel overwhelming. Left to our own devices we don't have the strength to persevere through difficult times. Thankfully, we don't have to. In this passage, we see that God's divine power has given us everything we need for life and godliness.

What does verse 3 say God's divine power comes through?

As we surrender to Jesus as Lord, we share in His divine nature and through Him, have an escape from the enticements and trouble that abound in the world. However, in order to take hold of this truth and the other great promises of God that we read throughout Scripture, *we must know Him.*

The word *knowledge* is mentioned repeatedly in 2 Peter 1:3–8 (four times if you're reading from the CSB translation). Knowing who He is, who has called us and equips us in our faith, is essential to endurance. To know God more, we must study His Word, be constant in prayer, and immerse ourselves in the things of God (i.e., worship, fellowship with other believers, serving others).

Take a moment and list the qualities found between verses 5 and 7:

How do these qualities help us? (Hint: see 2 Peter 1:8)

WHY WE ENDURE

Let's look one more time at **HEBREWS 12:2**,

Keeping our eyes on Jesus, the pioneer and perfecter of our faith. For the joy that lay before him, he endured the cross, despising the shame, and sat down at the right hand of the throne of God.

We are brought back to the perfect example of endurance we have in Jesus as we consider why we endure in faith to the end.

Read the verse again carefully. What lay before Jesus for which He would endure the cross?

The Bible tells us it is *joy*. What kind of joy you may ask? I would offer up that it is a multi-faceted joy. It entailed the joy of being obedient to what His Father asked of Him (Luke 22:42). It included the joy of laying His life down so that others would come to know God (Hebrews 2:10). It involved the joy of being at the right hand of the Father forever in eternity (Ephesians 1:20). That same joy awaits us as well, on the other side of our endurance.

Galatians 6:9 reads, "Let us not get tired of doing good, for we will reap at the proper time if we don't give up." When the Lord sees fit, we too will reap rewards from a generous Father. In the meantime, our responsibilities include running the race set before us, trusting in the promises of God, sharing the good news of the gospel of Jesus, and leaning into His provision of all we need for our endurance as Christians.

Endurance is not always easy, but we are called as believers to be ready to endure. We have within the family of faith countless others we can learn from about endurance. This includes the perfect example we have in Jesus. We do not endure in our own power, rather God empowers us to move through life steadfastly, and at the end of it all the greatest treasure awaits us in spending eternity with Jesus.

What does endurance look like for you today? Spend some time reflecting on these questions.

Where are you being asked to step out or persevere in faith?

What obstacles appear to be in your way?

What would it look like for you to choose joy and faith?

How has God already shown Himself faithful?

Take a moment to thank God for His daily provision of what you need to endure. Ask Him to continue to strengthen you with endurance for the work and the purpose He has called you to. Pray that He would help you persevere and be fruitful for His glory.

DAY 02

BE PATIENT IN SUFFERING

by Tessa Morrell

Suffering. Affliction. Pain. Sorrow. Heartache. These are words we are all acquainted with and yet I imagine we wish we didn't understand them so well. The reality is, to be human is to live with the tension of both joy and sorrow, beauty and pain, hope and suffering.

In John 16:33, amid some of Jesus's final words of encouragement for His disciples, He assured them (and us) that there would be suffering in this world. In some ways, this promise of suffering in life is discouraging. But I hope you'll see today that God can take our suffering and transform it into something beautiful for His glory and our good. This world is broken, and our trials are painful, but He can and will redeem all things.

READ JAMES 1:2-4.

²Consider it a great joy, my brothers and sisters, whenever you experience various trials, ³because you know that the testing of your faith produces endurance. ⁴And let endurance have its full effect, so that you may be mature and complete, lacking nothing.

THE BOOK OF JAMES

The book of James was most likely written by Jesus's brother. "Though he was not a follower of Christ during his earthly ministry (John 7:3-5), a post-resurrection appearance convinced James that Jesus is indeed the Christ (Acts 1:14; 1 Corinthians 15:7). James later led the Jerusalem church (Galatians 2:9, 12), exercising great influence there (Acts 1:14; 12:17; 15:13; 21:18; 1 Corinthians 15:7; Galatians 2:9, 12)."[3] He wrote his letter to early Christians to encourage them that "[t]rue faith must be lived out in everyday life by good deeds; such good works demonstrate the presence of faith and justification before God."[4]

What word might you replace "joy" with in verse 2, if you're being honest with yourself? Why is joy not often our first response when we experience suffering?

As we learn to endure and surrender our hearts to trust God in suffering, what does verse 4 say will happen to us?

Trials and joy don't seem to go together naturally. Trials and anger? Sure. Trials and despair? Absolutely. But trials and joy? How is that even possible? This is one of the many concepts that makes life as a follower of Jesus vastly different from life without Jesus. Our flesh—our natural inclinations, thoughts, and feelings—views suffering as a terrible thing. And without a doubt, all trials, whether they are "big" or "small," are painful. But for those who look to the Lord for His strength and trust His goodness and sovereignty, something unexpected and beautiful can happen in our hearts as we experience suffering. As we follow Jesus, we grow in our understanding of Him, His will and ways, and our place in His story. Maturity is a sign of that growth, and one of the ways God helps us mature in our faith is through suffering.

NEXT, LOOK UP AND READ ROMANS 5:1-5. What do you think it means to "boast in our afflictions"?

How does Romans 5:1-5 help you understand the process of maturity that happens through suffering?

Notice the last thing that is produced in us through affliction: hope. According to verse 5, this hope is not just wishful thinking. This is hope that cannot and will not ever disappoint us. God's love is what holds us together when we experience suffering. Our hope is firmly rooted in who He is and what He has done. His faithful presence with us through the Holy Spirit in every situation and season is what makes all the difference. In 2 Corinthians 4:16-18, we find this encouragement for the follower of Jesus,

> [16]*Therefore we do not give up. Even though our outer person is being destroyed, our inner person is being renewed day by day. [17]For our momentary light affliction is producing for us an absolutely incomparable eternal weight of glory. [18]So we do not focus on what is seen, but on what is unseen. For what is seen is temporary, but what is unseen is eternal.*

2 CORINTHIANS 4:16-18

Verse 16 is honest about the human experience—our earthly "outside" bodies grow older, weaker, and are "destroyed" throughout the course of our lives. We see and feel these effects on the daily. But as we learned earlier in James 1, God is at work on the inside—in our hearts—as we grow in our relationship with Him. He renews us day by day, and the maturity we gain through suffering is one way this happens.

> What can make it difficult to focus on the "unseen" in your daily life? What is one practical way you can "focus on what is unseen" today?

At the beginning of this day of study, I shared that Jesus was honest about the fact that we will endure suffering and trials in this world. But there's more. Jesus's full statement says this:

> *I have told you these things so that in me you may have peace. You will have suffering in this world.* ***Be courageous! I have conquered the world.***
>
> **JOHN 16:33** *(emphasis mine)*

Jesus has conquered the world. Everything that is broken. Every moment of unimaginable pain. Every disappointment and heartache and grief. When Jesus died and rose again, He proved that there is *nothing* in this world that is too strong for Him. And our suffering is no different. Jesus is *always* greater. I pray today that you will remember that in every moment God is with you, He loves you, and He will carry you through. The result of your suffering will be maturity, hope, and glory. Take things one day at a time, and trust Him. He is faithful.

Close today by writing a prayer to God about one area of your life that is painful or confusing right now. Be honest with Him about your suffering. Ask Him to grow and mature your faith in Him through it. Thank Him for His faithful love and presence, even on the hardest days.

DAY
03

LEAVE A
LEGACY

by Kelly D. King

Allyson Felix is the most decorated athlete in the World Athletics Championships, with twenty medals in track and field. Thirteen of those medals are from team relays. Yet, even as a track phenom, Allyson experienced the heartbreak of dropping the baton during a pass to teammate English Gardner in the 2016 Summer Olympics qualifying heat of the 4x100 relay. The first disqualification led to an appeal when Felix protested that another runner crossed into her lane, causing the mishap. The American team won the appeal, qualified in an unprecedented solo race, and then won the gold medal in the finals. It was the second fastest time recorded for that event, despite Gardner borrowing a pair of Felix's shoes.

Felix is a champion in track and field, but she is also outspoken about her faith in Christ and the influence of her father, a seminary professor, and her mother, a devoted Christian woman. "I am so blessed to have my family and the upbringing that I did. It means so much to me to have two very godly parents who both have so much wisdom. They are amazing role models that I have had the privilege to watch as I grew up."[5]

Felix knows how to physically pass a baton in a track race, but her parents displayed passing a baton of faith, an example of spiritual growth we see modeled throughout the Bible, and a practice every one of us can implement in our lives.

Look up the book of Judges in the Old Testament and **READ JUDGES 2:10-13.**

 THE BOOK OF JUDGES

The book of Judges is the second of the Historical Books in the Old Testament (Joshua–Esther). In the Hebrew Bible, these books are called the Former Prophets; the theological and spiritual concerns found in the Pentateuch (the first five books of the Bible) and the Prophets take precedence over simply recording historical facts. The book derives its name from the Hebrew designation of the principal characters, "shophetim" (2:16), which could also be translated as "governors." These judges were the Lord's agents of deliverance. The Lord is both the central character and the hero of Judges.[6]

One of the greatest leadership handoffs found in Scripture was between Moses and Joshua. In the last half of Numbers 27, the Lord reveals to Moses that Joshua would take his place. God had prepared Moses for forty years to take God's people into the Promised Land, and he had fulfilled his mission. Moses passed the baton to Joshua, but a dramatic shift happens after Joshua dies.

Look at Judges 2:10 and fill in the blanks.

After them another generation rose up _____ .

According to verses 11-13, what were the results?

v. 11: The Israelites _____ .

v. 11: They worshiped _____ .

v. 12: They abandoned _____ .

v. 12: They followed _____ .

v. 12: They angered _____ .

This unfortunate pattern is repeated in the time of Judges, much like a runner circling around a track and not learning how to correctly pass the baton of faith. Israel would reject God's plan, find themselves in slavery, and eventually call out to God for help. Salvation would come and peace would result. In God's mercies, even when the people dropped the baton of faith, God was there to pick them up.

Consider for a moment the cycle of faith in your own life. How was the gospel passed to you? Was it handed off smoothly from an earlier generation in your family or someone else? Draw a picture of each step you know from that cycle.

Take a moment to pause and thank the Lord for the person who shared Christ with you.

READ THE FOLLOWING VERSES FROM THE BOOK OF PSALMS.

⁴We will not hide them from their children,
but will tell a future generation
the praiseworthy acts of the Lord,
his might, and the wondrous works
he has performed.

⁵He established a testimony in Jacob
and set up a law in Israel,
which he commanded our ancestors
to teach to their children

⁶so that a future generation—
children yet to be born—might know.
They were to rise and tell their children

⁷so that they might put their confidence in God
and not forget God's works,
but keep his commands.

PSALM 78:4-7

One generation will declare your works to the next
and will proclaim your mighty acts.

PSALM 145:4

When faith is passed from one generation to the next, what things do we teach them about who God is? Fill in the blanks below.

PSALM 78:4:

Tell a future generation the _____ of the Lord, his _____, and the wondrous _____ he has performed.

PSALM 145:4:

One generation will declare _____ to the next and will proclaim _____.

We know it's important for faith to be passed down through generations, but the question remains: How are you making sure the next generation hears about God's faithfulness? Thankfully, the Bible doesn't only challenge us to live this way, it gives us examples of how to do this well.

LOOK UP 2 TIMOTHY IN THE NEW TESTAMENT, THEN READ 2 TIMOTHY 2:1-2 AND 2 TIMOTHY 4:6-8. From these two excerpts, what do you learn about modeling your faith for others?

2 TIMOTHY 2:1-2

2 TIMOTHY 4:6-8

Timothy had important role models in his life that passed their faith to him. As Paul is writing this letter to his young protégé, he reminds Timothy of two important women, both his grandmother and his mother, and how they were instrumental in his faith journey. You may or may not have children or grandchildren by birth, but each of us can have spiritual children.

Discipleship

When used in reference to the Christian life, this term describes the lifelong process of growing in one's relationship with Jesus.

In addition to making sure there is a clean hand off in a relay race, there is also a "takeover zone" that limits the length of the track wherein the pass must be completed. If one runner doesn't successfully make the transfer before the takeover zone ends, they are disqualified. As Paul finishes his letter, we see the takeover zone between the apostle and Timothy (see 2 Timothy 4:6-8). Paul understood his earthly race would be ending, but there was an eternal reward waiting that is much better than any earthly race. The end of his takeover zone was approaching, so he wanted to make sure he was handing off his faith to Timothy at the right time.

Whether you feel more like Timothy or Paul right now, think about your own legacy of faith. If you could shape your legacy, what would you want others to say about how you passed your faith to others?

CLOSE BY FLIPPING OVER TO THE NEXT NEW TESTAMENT BOOK—TITUS—AND READING ALL OF TITUS CHAPTER 2. As you read this chapter, look for some character traits you would like to emulate in your own life and write them down here.

Like Timothy, Titus was also a young leader whom Paul mentored. In this brief letter, Paul gives Titus practical and timely wisdom for the church's life. As a Gentile, Titus was an example of how Christianity was spreading throughout the Mediterranean world. Paul encouraged Titus to teach the church sound doctrine and Christlike behavior.

Regardless of how long you've been a Christian, now is always the right time to be investing in others and sharing your love for Jesus with them. What is the right next step for you to take toward passing the baton? Here are a few ideas. Pick one to start with, or add your own to the bottom of this list.

- Get more involved at church by volunteering or attending a small group.

- Commit to reading your Bible more and involve others with you.

- Find someone to invest in your spiritual growth.

- If you feel ready, find another (or two!) younger woman you can spend time with for the sake of sharing the gospel and encouraging her in discipleship.

Passing the baton of faith takes practice, intentionality, and a commitment to follow Christ each day. As you finish today's study, consider two or three younger women (or younger in the faith) that you can begin spending time with. Write down their names and start by praying for them. Whether it's your own children or younger women in the faith, consider how you can cheer them to pick up the baton and pass it on in the next leg of the relay of faith.

DAY 04

LIVE WITH COURAGE

by Cynthia Hopkins

Outside of the time my inner tube suddenly flipped upside down and my life flashed before my eyes on a rapid (not lazy) river water park ride, I never really thought a whole lot about death. I think that's the experience many of us have. We tend to avoid thoughts about death's very certain reality for as long as we can.

There comes a time for all of us, either because of our own circumstances or those of loved ones, when we can't ignore the reality any longer. For me, that time came suddenly. I had gone to the emergency room for an entirely unrelated medical issue and found out I had aneurysms in my brain. The year following that discovery included two brain surgeries and exponentially more thoughts and conversations about death than I had ever previously had. I can now say with confidence that my consideration of that topic was good, important, and long overdue.

Though it was largely unfamiliar territory for me, God's Word doesn't shy away from the topic. The Bible points our attention to death's reality from start to finish because what happens after is what matters most.

 ## THE BOOK OF ECCLESIASTES

The book of Ecclesiastes is one of the wisdom literature books of the Old Testament, along with Job, Psalms, Proverbs, and Song of Songs. The primary focus of Ecclesiastes is that the purpose of life is found in living for God alone.

READ THE FOLLOWING EXCERPT FROM THE BOOK OF ECCLESIASTES:

¹*There is an occasion for everything,*
and a time for every activity under heaven:

²*a time to give birth and a time to die;*
a time to plant and a time to uproot; . . .

¹⁴*I know that everything God does will last forever; there is no adding to it or taking from it. God works so that people will be in awe of him.*

ECCLESIASTES 3:1-2,14

As you know, life is always changing, and those changes are meant to have a point. Our lives operate in seasons and those seasons occur under God's authority and for His good purpose. That's true about every activity under heaven, even death.

Find Ecclesiastes 3 in your Bible and look through the list of occasions Solomon names in Ecclesiastes 3:1-8.

NOW READ VERSE 14 AGAIN. What purpose does God work to accomplish in death and every other occasion you face?

Why should the reality of death cause us to be in awe of God?

As certain as you are that there was a time for your birth, it is equally certain that there is a time for your death. Hebrews 9:27 puts it like this: "It is appointed for people to die once—and after this, judgment." Death is inevitable. Until Jesus returns, all of us will face it. And God has good purpose in this season for giving us knowledge of that season.

NOW LOOK UP AND READ 2 TIMOTHY 1:8-10. What facts does Paul lay out for us in these verses?

Put a star next to the fact that stands out to you the most as you think about death and dying. Why did you pick that one?

We don't know who wrote the book of Hebrews, another New Testament letter, but it's full of so many important truths about who Jesus is and who we are as His followers, including the following,

> *[14]Now since the children have flesh and blood in common, Jesus also shared in these, so that through his death he might destroy the one holding the power of death—that is, the devil— [15]and free those who were held in slavery all their lives by the fear of death.*

HEBREWS 2:14-15

Summarize these verses in your own words. What does the writer of Hebrews say about fearing death?

God's purpose for giving us the knowledge of death isn't that we would live in fear; it's that we would trust Jesus and walk through every season with Him in faith. Jesus brings the reality of every activity under heaven into light. And the reality of death is that Jesus has overcome it! Because Christ has defeated death, we don't have to be afraid. Yes, death is ugly and hard, but because of our victory in the risen Christ we have hope in what comes next—hope of eternity spent with Him. This hope is ours in "a time to die" (Ecclesiastes 3) and in every other time of life that precedes it.

CONSIDER THESE WORDS FROM PAUL'S LETTER TO THE ROMANS,

> *[7]For none of us lives for himself, and no one dies for himself. [8]If we live, we live for the Lord; and if we die, we die for the Lord. Therefore, whether we live or die, we belong to the Lord. [9]Christ died and returned to life for this: that he might be Lord over both the dead and the living.*

ROMANS 14:7-9

What does it mean that no one lives or dies for himself?

As you consider Paul's words in Romans 14:7-9, think back over the list of occasions in Ecclesiastes 3. Paul reminds us that whatever happens—tearing down, building, weeping, laughter, mourning, dancing, birth, death, or anything else—we belong to the Lord. That's huge!

It gives us the freedom to live for Christ no matter what we face. Jesus died and rose again to secure our place with Him in a kingdom that absolutely cannot be shaken.

If God's kingdom cannot be shaken, then neither can its kingdom citizens. Our security in Christ is meant to impact not only the life to come, but also the life that is right now. We belong to the Lord. So, let us live for the Lord—with abandon because He is Lord of the living and the dead. We are His, no matter what we face.

What would it look like for you to live "to the Lord" today?

READ THE FOLLOWING PASSAGES FROM TWO OF PAUL'S LETTERS,

²¹For me, to live is Christ and to die is gain. ²²Now if I live on in the flesh, this means fruitful work for me; and I don't know which one I should choose. ²³I am torn between the two. I long to depart and be with Christ—which is far better—²⁴but to remain in the flesh is more necessary for your sake.

PHILIPPIANS 1:21-24

⁶So we are always confident and know that while we are at home in the body we are away from the Lord. ⁷For we walk by faith, not by sight. ⁸In fact, we are confident, and we would prefer to be away from the body and at home with the Lord. ⁹Therefore, whether we are at home or away, we make it our aim to be pleasing to him.

2 CORINTHIANS 5:6-9

Based on these two passages, what happens to believers in Christ when they die?

What should be your perspective or purpose in every season of life?

When we die we will go to be with Jesus, but for now we live to please Him and do fruitful work for the kingdom. That doesn't mean we can't love the life we have on earth. It isn't bad to desire things in the physical world. After all, those are gifts from God. But if they become more important to us than Christ and His mission, then we have made idols out of them. The seasons Solomon wrote about in Ecclesiastes 3 aren't preeminent—Jesus is. God gives us the seasons of life so that we will be in awe of Him! That's why Paul held loosely to his own life and the things of the world; he knew the greater value of being with Christ in eternity. He reminds us to continually set our eyes on Jesus, knowing He is the reward both now and forever.

It's true. Death and dying are realities for every one of us. And God's Word encourages us to let the realities of that season shape this one. Will you? Will you live with courage because Jesus has defeated death? Will you step fully into His kingdom purposes no matter what you face? Believer in Christ, you belong to Him when you die, and you belong to Him now as you live—so let's live well.

Spend a few minutes in quiet reflection and prayer as you consider the purpose of the life God has given you and how to make the little time you have on this earth count for Him and His glory.

DAY
05

HOPE IN YOUR FUTURE

by Jaclyn S. Parrish

"IS EVERYTHING SAD GOING TO COME UNTRUE?"

—J.R.R. Tolkien[7]

I s Christianity worth it?

If you haven't asked yourself this question yet, you will. The Christian life is not an easy one, and there will come a point (probably several) when you'll wonder if the wages are worth the work. It's a hard question, but a fair one. So, is it worth it?

READ 1 CORINTHIANS 15.

Review 1 Corinthians 15:1-11. List the evidence Paul offers for Christ's resurrection in verses 1-11. Then list the proofs he offers for our own resurrection after death.

CHRIST'S RESURRECTION	OUR RESURRECTION

In this section from the apostle Paul's letter to the church in Corinth, Paul helps Christians then and now see the clear connection between the historical fact of Jesus's resurrection and the future hope we have in an eternity spent with Him. Christ died and rose again, not as a disembodied spirit, but as a person with a living, breathing body. Likewise, every person who is in Christ will live again after death, our bodies remade never to suffer or die again (1 Corinthians 15:20-28).

When you read about the future resurrection of believers, what are some of the questions you have?

What is the main point to cling to, despite all the things we can't know the answers to yet?

This promise of future resurrection and an eternity spent with God is the great hope of the Christian life, and as Paul makes clear, it all hinges on the veracity of Jesus's resurrection and the promise of ours. If Jesus was not raised from the dead, then we can't trust His claims of divinity, which means we can't trust that His life's sacrifice was sufficient to atone for our sins (1 Corinthians 15:17). If we can't look forward to a resurrection after death, then we have nothing to look forward to at all (vv. 18-19). And if our return to life after death doesn't come with vindication for our faith, then we've wasted our limited time doing work that wasn't worth it (vv. 30-32).

Like every one of us, the Corinthian church was a long way from what Christ required them to be. This church had factions to reunite and lawsuits to settle. They were confused about who should get married and who should stay single. Their worship services were chaos, people were getting drunk during the Lord's Supper, and then there was that one guy sleeping with his stepmother. These were not sudden, dramatic crises to be quickly weathered and soon forgotten. These were entrenched habits that would require daily, repeated, committed labor in order to overcome.

> Take some time to list out the things you know you'll need to do, to become, to give up, or to suffer in order to follow Christ. And be honest: Does He feel worth it?

NOW RE-READ 1 CORINTHIANS 15, AND PAY CAREFUL ATTENTION TO THE CHAPTER'S FINAL VERSE. Write a paraphrase of verse 58 here:

Notice what truths Paul returns to after fourteen chapters of imploring the Corinthians to be better. The hope of the resurrection is what empowers us to be steadfast and immovable in the cold, hard light of each new and laborious day. You can labor on, "because you know that your labor in the Lord is not in vain" (v. 58).

NOW TURN TO THE VERY BACK OF YOUR BIBLE AND READ THE LAST TWO CHAPTERS, REVELATION 21–22. As you read, note any words and imagery that stand out to you about the beauty and value of the new creation.

The end times. Over the years, both the church and pop culture have attempted to capture what the end of life as we know it might be like. But Scripture is not terribly forthcoming on the details of Christ's return and the restoration of our broken world. What we do know, though, is here in Revelation 21–22. The Revelation of John ends with "the holy city, the new Jerusalem, coming down out of heaven from God" (Revelation 21:2). God does not exile us from the home He made for us in Genesis 1. He makes His home with us (21:3). Christ does not bring all things to an end. He makes all things new (21:5).

> **READ 1 CORINTHIANS 3:5-15.** What does Paul mean by the "work" referenced in verses 13-15?

Whatever fire comes at the end of time is not a blast of napalm, but the heat of the kiln, a purifying flame that cleanses an artwork of its impurities and perfects the final display. Your daily labor—be it evangelizing strangers, changing diapers, befriending neighbors, caring for an aging parent, teaching children, or performing surgeries—is an investment in the New Creation that will one day cover a new earth. In the words of Christian painter Makoto Fujimura, "what we build, design, and depict on this side of eternity matters, because in some mysterious way, those creations will become a part of the future city of God."[8] With Christ as our foundation, we can build our lives with confidence, trusting that the quality of our work will be proven in the end.

Remember, you are made in God's image, made to joyfully give and thankfully receive goodness, truth, and beauty. That didn't stop when sin entered the world, and it won't stop when sin leaves the world.

Review your notes from the last twenty-five days of study. Now take a few moments to simply marvel and thank God for the new life you have now and forever in Christ.

REFLECT

Take a few minutes to reflect on the truths you uncovered in your study of God's Word this week. Journal any final thoughts below, or use the space to take notes during your Bible study group conversation. The three questions on the opposite page can be used for your personal reflection or group discussion.

Leading a group? Download the *Alive* leader guide at **lifeway.com/alive**.

As you reflect on the Bible passages you read this week, what stands out to you about the character of God?

How have you been challenged and encouraged in your relationship with Jesus through what you've learned?

Write down one way you can use what you've learned this week to encourage someone else.

BECOMING A CHRISTIAN

Romans 10:17 says, "So faith comes from what is heard, and what is heard comes through the message about Christ."

Maybe you've stumbled across new information in this study. Or maybe you've attended church all your life, but something you read here struck you differently than it ever has before. If you have never accepted Christ but would like to, read on to discover how you can become a Christian.

Your heart tends to run from God and rebel against Him. The Bible calls this sin. Romans 3:23 says, "For all have sinned and fall short of the glory of God."

Yet God loves you and wants to save you from sin, to offer you a new life of hope. John 10:10b says, "I have come so that they may have life and have it in abundance."

To give you this gift of salvation, God made a way through His Son, Jesus Christ. Romans 5:8 says, "But God proves his own love for us in that while we were still sinners, Christ died for us."

You receive this gift by faith alone. Ephesians 2:8-9 says, "For you are saved by grace through faith, and this not from yourselves; it is God's gift—not from works, so that no one can boast."

Faith is a decision of your heart demonstrated by the actions of your life. Romans 10:9 says, "If you confess with your mouth, 'Jesus is Lord,' and believe in your heart that God raised him from the dead, you will be saved."

If you trust that Jesus died for your sins and want to receive new life through Him, pray a prayer similar to the following to express your repentance and faith in Him:

Dear God, I know I am a sinner. I believe Jesus died to forgive me of my sins. I accept Your offer of eternal life. Thank You for forgiving me of all my sins. Thank You for my new life. From this day forward, I will choose to follow You.

If you have trusted Jesus for salvation, please share your decision with your group leader or another Christian friend. If you are not already attending church, find one in which you can worship and grow in your faith. Following Christ's example, ask to be baptized as a public expression of your faith.

ENDNOTES

WEEK ONE

1. Robert D. Bergen, "Genesis," in *CSB Study Bible: Notes*, ed. Edwin A. Blum and Trevin Wax (Nashville: Holman Bible Publishers, 2017), 1.

2. Allen P. Ross, *Creation and Blessing: A Guide to the Study and Exposition of the Book of Genesis*, (Grand Rapids: Baker Book House, 1988), 113–114.

3. D. A. Neal and John Anthony Dunne, "Eden, Garden of," in *The Lexham Bible Dictionary*, ed. John D. Barry et al. (Bellingham: Lexham Press, 2016).

4. Charles L. Quarles, "Paul," *Holman Illustrated Bible Dictionary*, ed. Chad Brand et al., (Nashville: Holman Bible Publishers, 2003), 1254.

5. Edwin A. Blum, "Romans," in *CSB Study Bible: Notes*, 1777.

6. *Merriam-Webster.com Dictionary*, s.v., "righteous," accessed October 12, 2023, https://www.merriam-webster.com/dictionary/righteous.

7. Walter Kaiser Jr., "Jeremiah," in *CSB Study Bible: Notes*, 1137.

8. F. B. Huey Jr., Jeremiah, *Lamentations*, vol. 16, The New American Commentary (Nashville: Broadman & Holman Publishers, 1993), 24.

9. Jerry M. Henry, "Trinity," in *Holman Illustrated Bible Dictionary*, 1625.

10. Jack P. Lewis, "Gentiles," in *Holman Illustrated Bible Dictionary*, 638.

11. R. K. Harrison, "Abraham," in *Holman Illustrated Bible Dictionary*, 10–14.

12. Peter Toon, "Righteousness," in *Evangelical Dictionary of Biblical Theology*, electronic ed., Baker Reference Library (Grand Rapids: Baker Book House, 1996), 687.

13. Leon Morris, "Justification," in *Evangelical Dictionary of Biblical Theology*, 441.

14. Andrew H. Trotter Jr., "Atonement," in *Evangelical Dictionary of Biblical Theology*, 44.

15. Anna Ptaszynski, "463: No Such Thing As An Especially Attractive Barge," January 26, 2023, in *No Such Thing As A Fish*, podcast, , https://www.nosuchthingasafish.com/.

16. Jason C. Kuo, "Ephesians, Letter to the," in *The Lexham Bible Dictionary*.

17. *Merriam-Webster's Unabridged Dictionary*, s.v. "grace," accessed October 12, 2023, https://unabridged.merriam-webster.com/unabridged/grace.

18. *Oxford Languages*, s.v. "grace" https://www.google.com/search?q=grace.

WEEK TWO

1. *Merriam-Webster's Unabridged Dictionary*, s.v. "receive," accessed October 12, 2023, https://unabridged.merriam-webster.com/unabridged/receive.

2. *Merriam-Webster.com Dictionary*, s.v. "believe," accessed October 12, 2023, https://www.merriam-webster.com/dictionary/believe.

3. Trent C. Butler, "David," in *Holman Illustrated Bible Dictionary*, 391.

4. Kevin R. Warstler, "Psalms," in *CSB Study Bible: Notes*, 816.

5. Paul Jackson, "Holy Spirit," in *Holman Illustrated Bible Dictionary*, 773.

6. Stanley J. Grenz and Jay T. Smith, *Pocket Dictionary of Ethics*, The IVP Pocket Reference Series (Downers Grove: InterVarsity Press, 2003), 69.

7. "Music: Fiddler's Will," *TIME*, October 19, 1953, https://content.time.com/time/subscriber/article/0,33009,823088,00.html

8. Andrew Wilson, *1 Corinthians for You*, God's Word for You Commentary Series (United Kingdom: Good Book Company, 2021), 135.

9. Stephen T. Um, *1 Corinthians: The Word of the Cross,* Preaching the Word Commentary Series (Wheaton: Crossway, 2015), 215–216.

10. Thomas Schreiner, "The Gifts of the Spirit," *The Gospel Coalition*, accessed October 12, 2023, https://www.thegospelcoalition.org/essay/the-gifts-of-the-spirit/

WEEK THREE

1. F. Alan Tomlinson, "1 Corinthians," in *CSB Study Bible: Notes*, 1810.

2. Johnnie Godwin, "Baptism," *Holman Bible Dictionary*, ed. Trent C. Butler, (Nashville: Broadman & Holman, 1991), accessed October 12, 2023, https://www.studylight.org/dictionaries/eng/hbd/b/baptism.html.

3. James Leo Garrett, *Systematic Theology*, (Eugene, OR: Wipf and Stock, 2014), 503.

4. Craig Blomberg, Matthew, vol. 22, *The New American Commentary* (Nashville: Broadman & Holman Publishers, 1992), 81.

5. Charles L. Quarles, "Matthew," in *CSB Study Bible: Notes*, 1553.

6. Garrett, *Systematic Theology*, 521.

7. "The History Behind 7 Passover Traditions," *TIME*, April 4, 2023, accessed October 12, 2023, https://time.com/5188494/passover-history-traditions/.

8. N.T. Wright and Michael F. Bird, *The New Testament in Its World: An Introduction to the History, Literature, and Theology of the First Christians*, (Grand Rapids: Zondervan, 2019), 252–256.

9. Claude L. Howe Jr., "Ordinances," in *Holman Illustrated Bible Dictionary*, 1230.

10. Ibid.

11. Garrett, *Systematic Theology*, 611–614.

12. *Tyndale Bible Dictionary*, Tyndale Reference Library, ed. Walter A. Elwell and Philip Wesley Comfort, (Wheaton: Tyndale House Publishers, 2001), 1311.

13. Ibid, 1060.

14. Strong's G2657, *Blue Letter Bible*, accessed October 12, 2023, https://www.blueletterbible.org/lexicon/g2657/csb/tr/0-1/.

15. R. E. Glaze, "2 Corinthians," *Holman Bible Dictionary*, accessed October 12, 2023, https://www.studylight.org/dictionaries/eng/hbd/2/2-corinthians.html.

16. Strong's G2431, *Blue Letter Bible*, accessed October 12, 2023, https://www.blueletterbible.org/lexicon/g2431/csb/mgnt/0-1/.

17. David W. Music, "Doxology," *Holman Bible Dictionary*, accessed October 12, 2023, https://www.studylight.org/dictionaries/enghbd/d/doxology.html.

WEEK FOUR

1. Randy Hatchett, "Prayer," Holman Bible Dictionary, accessed October 26, 2023, https://www.studylight.org/dictionaries/hbd/p/prayer.html

2. Millard Erickson, *Christian Theology: Second Edition*, (Grand Rapids: Baker Books, 1998), 311.

3. Stuart K. Weber, "Matthew," *Holman New Testament Commentary*, ed. Max Anders, (Nashville: Broadman & Holman Publishers, 2000).

4. *The Baptist Faith & Message*, (Southern Baptist Convention, 2000), accessed October 26, 2023, https://bfm.sbc.net/bfm2000/#i.

5. Vine, W. "Sin (Noun and Verb) - Vine's Expository Dictionary of New Testament Words." *Blue Letter Bible*. Last Modified June 24, 1996, https://www.blueletterbible.org/search/Dictionary/viewTopic.cfm?topic=VT0002638.

6. John Piper, "Glorifying God," Campus Outreach Staff Conference, July 15, 2013, Orlando, FL, transcript, https://www.desiringgod.org/messages/glorifying-god-period.

WEEK FIVE

1. *Merriam-Webster's Unabridged Dictionary*, s.v. "endurance," accessed October 26, 2023, https://unabridged.merriam-webster.com/unabridged/endurance.

2. Malcolm B. Yarnell III, "Hebrews," in *CSB Study Bible: Notes*, 1945.

3. R. Gregg Watson, "James," in *CSB Study Bible: Notes*, 1964.

4. "Introduction to James," *Lifeway Women's Bible*, (Nashville: Holman Bible Publishers, 2022), 1781.

5. Gregory Tomlin, "OLYMPICS: Runner Allyson Felix," *Christian Examiner*, August 10, 2016, http://www.christianexaminer.com/article/olympic-runner-allyson-felix-tells-reporters-faith-leads-my-life/50954.htm.

6. Iain M. Duguid, "Judges," in *CSB Study Bible: Notes*, 359.

7. J.R.R. Tolkien, *The Return of the King*, (United Kingdom: HarperCollins Publishers, 2001) 930.

8. Makoto Fujimura, *Art and Faith: A Theology of Making*, (New Haven: Yale University Press, 2020), 12.

CONTRIBUTORS

TINA BOESCH

Tina Boesch serves as manager of the Lifeway Women Bible Studies team. She earned an MA in Theology at Regent College in Vancouver, British Columbia. For fourteen years, she and her husband and their three kids called Istanbul, Turkey, home. Now they've settled north of Nashville, but she still misses steaming cups of Turkish tea. Tina is the author of *Given: The Forgotten Meaning and Practice of Blessing.*

Y BONESTEELE

Y Bonesteele is the editor for *The Gospel Project* Adult Bible Study curriculum and has an MDiv. with an emphasis on evangelism and discipleship from Talbot School of Theology. She lived on mission in Madrid, Spain for seven years with her husband and four kids. Today, she resides in Middle Tennessee and enjoys giving out flowers from her garden or cookies from her kitchen to neighbors and strangers.

MISSIE BRANCH

Missie Branch serves as VP of Community Engagement at Stand For Life. She is married to Duce Branch and together they have four children. Missie is a contributing author to The Whole Woman: Ministering to Her Heart, Soul, Mind, and Strength and Women & Work: Bearing God's Image and Joining in His Mission Through Our Work. She is also the co-host of the Women & Work Podcast.

EUNICE J. CHUNG CARLSON

Eunice J. Chung Carlson is a professor of Bible & Theology at Liberty University. A Virginia native, she is a proud graduate of the University of Virginia (Wahoowa!). She completed her PhD at the Southern Baptist Theological Seminary in biblical spirituality. When not teaching and writing, Eunice is spending time with her family and friends, reading, finding a great bakery, or walking in the woods.

YANA JENAY CONNER

Yana Jenay Conner is a writer and Bible teacher who seeks to help others think well about faith and culture. Yana earned an MDiv in Christian Ministry from Southeastern Baptist Theological Seminary and now serves as the Discipleship Director at Vertical Church. She is also an avid writer and hosts a podcast called *Living Single.* You can find more of her writing and teaching at yanajenay.com.

ERIN FRANKLIN

Erin Franklin is a marketing specialist on the Lifeway Women team. A graduate of Lipscomb University, she enjoys a good ping-pong match, photography, and learning new things. You can connect with her on Instagram @erin_franklin.

AMY-JO GIRARDIER

Amy-Jo Girardier loves how God uniquely makes people and generations for His glory. She is the Women's Minister and has served for over twenty years at Brentwood Baptist in Brentwood, Tennessee. She is an author of three Lifeway Bible studies and loves writing resources for teen girls and women. Amy-Jo loves getting to serve with her husband Darrel on staff and being with their two boys. You can find her on Instagram: @amyjogirardier.

ASHLEY MARIVITTORI GORMAN

Ashley Marivittori Gorman serves as a senior acquisitions editor at B&H Publishing Group. She holds an MDiv from Southeastern Theological Seminary and has been trained under The Charles Simeon Trust. Ashley and her husband, Cole, live in Nashville, Tennessee, with their daughter and son. You can find her writing in Lifeway Women Bible studies, books like *World on Fire*, and on digital venues like *The Gospel Coalition*, *ERLC*, and *Christ and Culture*.

MICHELLE R. HICKS

Michelle R. Hicks is the managing editor for *Journey* devotional magazine and serves on the leadership training team with Lifeway Women. Her prayer is for women to grow closer to Jesus every day through His Word.

CYNTHIA HOPKINS

Cynthia Hopkins is a longtime writer of Bible studies, devotions, and articles across all age groups from students through senior adults. She now serves in that capacity on Lifeway's custom content and short term studies team—remotely from The Woodlands, Texas. Cynthia is exceedingly grateful for that work and the many other ways God shows Himself to her!

ELIZABETH HYNDMAN

Elizabeth Hyndman is the editorial project leader for Lifeway Women Academy and cohosts the *MARKED* podcast. A Nashville native, grammarian, traveler, and tea drinker, Elizabeth can be found on Instagram and Twitter @edhyndman.

KELLY D. KING

Kelly D. King is the Women's Minister at Quail Springs Baptist Church in Oklahoma City, Oklahoma. She is the former manager of Magazines/Devotional Publishing and Women's Ministry Specialist for Lifeway Christian Resources. She has a Doctorate of Ministry degree from Gateway Seminary. Her favorite things are spending time in Colorado at her family cabin and being KK to her grandchildren.

CONTRIBUTORS

NIKKI LAWRENCE

Nikki Lawrence is a Marketing Executive at a Fortune 500 Company and often serves as a Mistress of Ceremony at conferences, fundraisers, and events across the country. Her passion is to see women walk boldly in whatever God has called them into. In her free time, she can be found daydreaming of home decor, road tripping with friends, or playing with her niece and nephews.

BLAIR LINNE

Blair Linne is a Bible teacher, author, actress, and Christian spoken word artist. Blair has toured globally and is known as one of the originators of the Christian Spoken Word genre. Proclaiming the gospel of Jesus Christ through speaking and spoken word is her passion. She lives in Portland with her husband Shai Linne and their three children.

TESSA MORRELL

Tessa Morrell is a production editor for Lifeway Women. She is passionate about serving in her church and studying Scripture with others. She also enjoys visiting local coffee shops, browsing antique stores for hours, and creating art of all kinds.

JACLYN S. PARRISH

Jaclyn S. Parrish is the Director of Marketing at Southwestern Seminary in Fort Worth, TX. She holds a BA in English and Christian Studies from Dallas Baptist University and an M.A. in Religion from the B.H. Carroll Theological Institute. She has served in local churches and Southern Baptist entities for over a decade, and has written for *The Gospel Coalition*, *Christianity Today*, and *Love Thy Nerd*.

CHRISTINE THORNTON

Christine Thornton desires to help the church mature as Christians grow in clarity of the gospel and the ability to effectively communicate it to one another and the world. She currently serves as assistant professor of Christian Thought and director of the Master of Theology program at Southeastern Baptist Theological Seminary. She has contributed to *The Gospel Coalition*, *Christianity Today*, and numerous other publications.

MARY WILEY

Mary Wiley is the author of *Everyday Theology* and *Discover the Bible: A Kid's Guide to Reading and Understanding God's Word*. She serves as the associate publisher for B&H Publishing Group. She holds a BA in Christian studies and English from the University of Mobile and an MA in theological studies from The Southern Baptist Theological Seminary. She and her husband, John, have three children and live in the Nashville area.

Explore the stories of more than 30 women in Scripture whose lives have inspired generations of women in their faith and devotion to God. (6 sessions)

Bible Study Book
$16.99 • 005841037
lifeway.com/devoted

Develop a thankful heart that can be cultivated into a continual harvest of gratitude, regardless of the circumstances. (4 sessions)

Bible Study Book
$16.99 • 005841132
lifeway.com/grateful

MORE STUDIES BY LIFEWAY WOMEN

Focusing on the events and deeper theological meaning of the Passion Week, this study will not only help the reader understand how beautifully deep Christ's sacrifice for us was, but also how to live in light of these life-giving truths.

Bible Study Book
005826669 $12.99
lifeway.com/easterstudy

800.458.2772

Pricing and availability subject to change without notice.

Lifeway. women

Get the most from your study.

In this study, you'll:

- Discover what it means to be a follower of Jesus, find your identity in Christ, and be part of His church.

- Grasp a deeper understanding of Biblical truths that the Christian life rests upon.

- Lay a strong spiritual foundation for a lifetime of following Jesus.

- Strengthen your walk with Christ whether you've been following Him for days or decades.

Browse study formats, a free session sample, a leader guide, church promotional materials, and more at

lifeway.com/alive